SECRET
BRUSSELS

Nathalie Capart, Isabelle de Pange,
Nicolas van Beek, Florent Verstraeten
and Jean-Jacques & Brigitte Evrard-Lauwereins

JONGLEZ PUBLISHING

Travel guides

Nathalie Capart has lived in Brussels since she was old enough to head out on her own. A lover of words who has worked with text for many years, she has branched out, losing herself and finding her way, guided above all by her curiosity and her enthusiasm, with a strong preference for exotic trips to the next street over.

Isabelle de Pange was born in Uccle and lives in Schaerbeek. She is an art historian (at UCL) and an architecture enthusiast. She worked at the Inventaire du Patrimoine Architectural Bruxelles-Capitale (Monument Heritage Brussels) for several years before becoming head curator at Musées de la Ville de Bruxelles (Brussels City Museums) from 2015 to 2018. She has authored several works about her hometown.

Florent Verstraeten was born and grew up in Brussels. Curious about everything, he paces the city, always looking for the most secret spots that even the inhabitants don't know. In his free time, he organizes bicycle or pedestrian tours in various districts of Brussels. His ambition: to awaken the desire to walk around in our own city and reclaim it.

Graphic designers by trade, **Jean-Jacques & Brigitte Evrard-Lauwereins** have lived in Brussels for over 50 years. Lovers of art and architecture, in 2020 they started their admirable-facades.brussels website, which presents more than 300 remarkable buildings in Brussels.

Secret Brussels is the result of our observation that only a selection of guides tending to describe the same familiar places are available to residents or frequent visitors to the Belgian capital. They don't offer much of a surprise or insight to someone who knows the city fairly well.

This guide is aimed at such readers, although we hope it will also appeal to the occasional visitor who'd like a change from the tourist itineraries.

Comments on the guide or information on places we may not have mentioned are more than welcome and will help us to improve future editions.

Don't hesitate to contact us:
Jonglez Publishing,
E-mail: info@jonglezpublishing.com

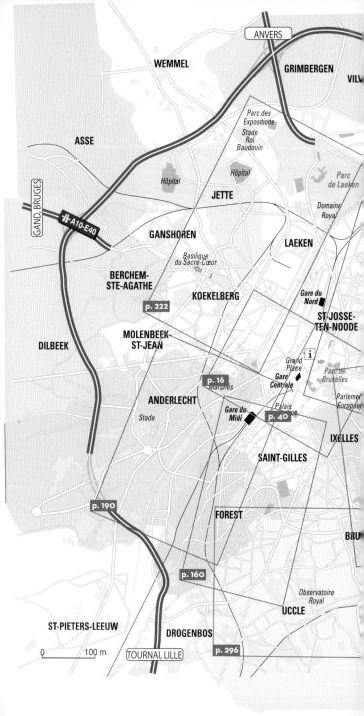

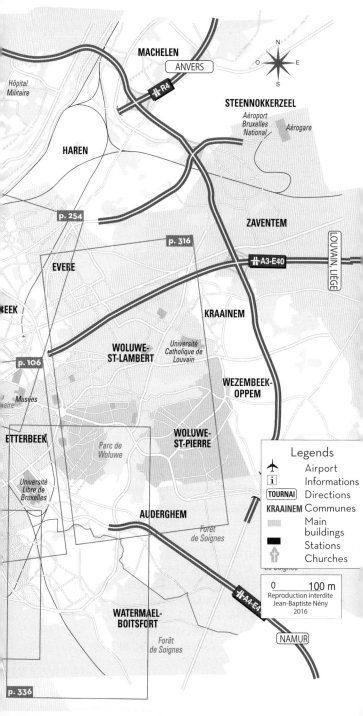

CONTENTS

Centre West of the Boulevards

Centre East of the Boulevards

Ixelles, Etterbeek, European District

CONTENTS

Saint-Gilles and Forest

Anderlecht

CONTENTS

Molenbeek, Koekelberg, Laeken

Schaerbeek, Saint-Josse-Ten-Noode

Uccle

CONTENTS

Woluwe Saint-Pierre and Woluwe Saint-Lambert

Auderghem and Watermael-Boitsfort

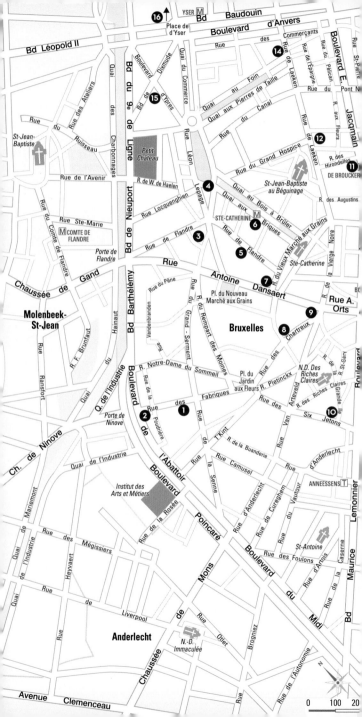

Centre West of the Boulevards

SHOT TOWER

This is not a chimney

Rue des Fabriques 54
Open erratically 9am–5pm
Tram No. 18 or 82, Porte de Ninove stop

© Jean-Jacques Evrard

From a distance, the Tour à Plombs (shot tower) looks like the average factory chimney, of which there are a fair number in Brussels. Basically nothing special. However, this chimney is not what it seems but is the last tower of its kind in continental Europe.

Built about 1885 by the foundry of Pelgrims and Bombeeck, the tower was used until the 1940s to make lead shot by a remarkable process invented in 1792 by William Watts of Bristol (UK).

Access to the top of the tower, 55 m in height and 5 m in diameter, used to be by a spiral staircase lit by embrasures. In poor condition and inaccessible nowadays, this staircase can, however, be seen by craning your head inside the tower, avoiding the droppings of the resident pigeons.

At the top of the tower, lead was heated in a furnace in the base of which were little holes. The molten lead fell in the form of little droplets which, during the 55 m fall cooled by more than 300°C by the time they reached the bottom.

Caught at the end of their fall in a tank full of sulphite, the solidified 'drops' were machined, calibrated and coated in graphite to be ready for use in hunting.

Although classified as a historic monument in 1984, the tower today is in a poor state. It is now within the grounds of an annex of the department of Arts and Crafts used by dentistry, optometry and nursing students.

Ring the bell vigorously at a reasonable hour. One of the wardens will open the door and, if you ask politely enough, may let you have a closer view of this dinosaur of the golden age of industry.

It is nevertheless perfect for romantics, who will take much pleasure in strolling around this remarkable industrial relic while trying to imagine it as it was at the height of its activity.

MAGRITTE'S PHYSIOGNOMICAL FOUNTAIN

Find the painter's face

Place de Ninove

© Jean-Jacques Evrard

On Place de Ninove, nothing clashes with the humdrum Brussels routine – not the rows of neoclassical houses, not the old trees, and especially not the blue stone fountain gracing the centre of the square. And yet, if you look closely at the moulded base of the fountain, which seems rather ordinary at first, you'll see a double profile emerge in the negative on both sides, delimited at each end by the thin stream of water falling from the basin.

Perhaps you recognize him? It is Magritte's face that is so skilfully depicted here in a manner dear to Luca Maria Patella, the artist behind this work placed here in 2002. The inventor of 'physiognomical vases',

this Italian artist has already sculpted the profiles of the likes of Goethe, Diderot, Duchamp and Annunzio in marble using the same technique (to learn more, visit his 'official and unofficial site': http://lucapatella.altervista.org/index-english.htm). But here, he has surpassed himself: what better homage could be paid to the painter of mysteries than this ghostly apparition that haunts an ordinary local fountain?

NEARBY
Rue de la Cigogne ③
Rue de Flandre 138–140 and Rue du Rempart des Moines 23
The rue de la Cigogne is probably one of the prettiest lanes in Brussels. Repaved in original cobbles and lined by old houses, it has a rustic charm much to the liking of its residents. On the street side of rue du Rempart des Moines, the way in is through the gateway of a attractive little chapel, in which there is a statue of St Roch dating from 1780 by an unknown sculptor.

STATUE OF THE 'SOLDIER' PIGEON ④

A patriotic pigeon

Square des Blindés
Metro Sainte-Catherine

Belgium is surely the only country in the world to possess a statue in honour of soldier pigeons. The result of a strong pigeon-fancying tradition that was already widespread before 1939 (130,000 adherents at the beginning of the century), Belgium was the only country to use racing pigeons for military purposes in the Second World War. This tradition probably owes something to the large working-class population of the Charleroi district: with their limited means, the workers found in keeping pigeons a pastime that allowed them a measure of escapism at little expense.

With the rise in the standard of living, the number of pigeon-fanciers dropped (18,000 today), but they still organize competitions, which have become the mainstay of this hobby. The 50 or so countries with pigeon clubs thus meet regularly to release their birds, which often have to fly distances of 1,500 km.

At the offices of the *Royale Fédération Colombophile Belge*, 39 rue de Livourne, Ixelles, you will find a secretariat delighted to answer any questions, as well as a few pigeons in the garden.

The racing pigeon

Whether released at 500 m or 100 km from home, even in certain cases over 1,000 km, the racing pigeon has that fantastic ability to always know its way back.

Even if the reason for these exceptional skills is still unknown, some people attribute the gift to the presence of tiny crystals in the brain. This trait was detected a long time ago, notably by Julius Caesar who, during the invasion of Gaul, used homing pigeons to send messages back to Rome to inform headquarters of his campaign's progress.

On the other hand, so there'll be no misunderstanding: the pigeon that you sometimes see at the cinema, which is released and asked to take a message somewhere and then return, doesn't exist.

The pigeon is only (so to speak) capable of returning home. This is why, in order to send a message to several places, pigeons raised at each destination have to be taken out.

To send several successive messages to the same place, the requisite number of pigeons have to be taken out. There's nothing miraculous in the voyage, but it would be difficult to receive messages with the pigeons moving from dovecote to dovecote.

LA BELLONE, HOUSE OF PERFORMING ARTS

Hidden from the street, one of the most beautiful façades in Brussels

Rue de Flandre 46
02 513 33 33
bellone.be
Monday 9am–3pm and Tuesday to Friday 9am–5pm
Metro Sainte-Catherine

Hidden from the street and therefore little known by most citizens, the La Bellone possesses one of the most beautiful façades in the capital. Now converted into a centre dedicated to the performing arts, it houses a number of associations such as Contredanse, Les Midis de la Poésie (poetry readings, conferences), a library, rehearsal room, and meeting rooms. Unfortunately, it puts on shows only too rarely, although dinner-dances, conferences and other activities let people enjoy this architectural marvel.

It is also possible to have a quick look around if you go in office hours: Monday to Friday from 10am to 6pm. Stay unobtrusive and you'll be left in peace for a while to enjoy this façade built between 1697 and 1708 by Jean Cosyn, an architect and sculptor who took part in the reconstruction of Brussel's Grand-Place from 1695.

Take a copy of the explanatory brochure at the entrance and look out for the many details such as the bust of Bellone, goddess of war in ancient Rome, who lends her name to the building. It is encircled by a panoply of weapons and banners.

Built on a plot of land belonging to the former convent of the White Sisters of the Rose of Jericho, the Bellone is bursting with Christian symbolism. The twelve windows associate the twelve months of the year and the twelve apostles. The number seven is repeated many times: there are seven rods in the fasces representing the law at the base of the third pilaster to the left of the door; the cock on the base of the first pilaster to the right of the door bears seven tail feathers; the lintel of the main doorway is decorated with seven triangular 'beads'; finally the pilasters themselves are decorated with seven parallel grooves.

It must have been raining when the idea of roofing over the internal courtyard saw the light of day. This was done in 1995 and people can now benefit from this gem whatever the weather. It's just a pity that it rains so much, as we would have preferred to see the façade free to breath, like a living reminder of the past.

Unfortunately, today it sometimes feels like being in a museum.

NEARBY
Quai aux Briques 62 (6)

This house, a prime example of 17th-century architecture, has a beautiful Baroque-style door topped by a small round window and a keystone depicting a boat – a reminder of the fact that the Sainte-Catherine district used to be a harbour, as ponds once connected it directly to the Willebroek canal. The ponds were filled in during the 19th century.

FRIEZE WITH A MOTIF OF BANANAS AND ORANGES

Architectural remains from the colonial era

Rue Antoine Dansaert 75–79 – Rue du Vieux Marché aux Grains 7-9-11

In addition to the Gran Eldorado room at the UGC de Brouckère (see p. 30), the decoration of some buildings in the centre of Brussels is inspired by the flora and fauna of the former Belgian Congo (now the Democratic Republic of Congo), and in particular the banana.

The finest example is the building at nos. 75 to 79 Rue Antoine Dansaert, on the corner of Rue du Vieux Marché aux Grains (nos. 7, 9 and 11).

Built in 1927 by Eugène Dhuicque for exotic fruit wholesaler Gérard Koninckx Frères, its top two floors feature a magnificent, enamelled,

stoneware frieze. Designed by Armand Paulis and executed by the Parisian ceramist Dhomme, it depicts several magnificent motifs of bananas (with their characteristic large leaves) and oranges (still hanging from the trees), fruits that made the fortunes of many merchants in the early 20th century.

The building was listed in 1998.

Two other Gérard Koninckx Frères buildings

Gérard Koninckx Frères owned two other buildings in the district: one at Nos. 22 and 23 on the Place du Nouveau Marché aux Grains and the other with pretty pilasters featuring bananas and oranges (see p. 36) at nos. 32 and 34 on the Boulevard d'Ypres.

ZINNEKE-PIS

8

With the Manneken-Pis and his wife Jeanneke-Pis, the family is complete

Corner of rue des Chartreux and rue du Vieux Marché aux Grains
Metro Bourse

© Jean-Jacques Evrard

Superb and self-mocking, this is just a statue of a dog urinating. With the famous Manneken-Pis and his wife Jeanneke-Pis near the rue des Bouchers, the family is complete.

Its creator, Tom Frantzen, has made a speciality of urban sculptures based on Belgian popular culture. In Place Sainctelette the Vaartkapoen ('Canal Guy', i.e. young rascal from Molenbeek on the other side of the canal) appears from a drain to grab a police officer, who is wearing badge No. 15 in homage to Hergé's Quick and Flupke. Also, at the corner of rue du Midi and rue des Moineaux (not far from the Zinneke-Pis), is the sculpture of 'Madame Chapeau', the famous character from *Bossemans et Coppenolle*, a vaudeville theatre sketch on the misunderstandings between two families who supported rival football teams: the Union Saint-Gilloise and the Daring Club de Bruxelles.

NEARBY
Café Greenwich toilets   ⑨
Rue des Chartreux 7
Built in 1914, the well-known Café Greenwich, rendezvous of the city's chess players, possesses a very fine, original interior (completed in 1916), which gives it a pleasant and authentic feeling, probably little changed from the time when Magritte apparently frequented the café. Less well-known on the other hand are the superb toilets in the basement, also original. Well worth a visit.

Institut Technique Annessens-Funck   ⑩
Rue de la Grande Île 39
02 510 07 50
Built in 1905 by the architect E. van Acker, the Annessens Institute has a beautiful Art Nouveau façade that you could easily imagine coming

straight out of a Schuiten and Peeters comic strip or a science-fiction film. Formerly belonging to Papeteries de Belgique, this concrete edifice took on its current educational function in 1949. The entrance hall is also decorated with ceramics.

© Jean-Jacques Evrard

GRAN ELDORADO ROOM OF THE UGC CINEMA OF BROUCKÈRE

Impressions of Africa: an Art Deco cinema complete with jungle decor and elephant's head

Place De Brouckère 38
09 00 10 440
Metro De Brouckère

While the UGC De Brouckère cinema complex is obviously well known, the magnificent Gran Eldorado cinema is too often forgotten. Overwhelmed by the twelve theatres making up the complex, this 700-seat cinema is an Art Deco gem. Built between 1931 and 1933 by the Liege architect Marcel Chabot, it was formerly part of the Eldorado that merged with La Scala in 1974. After a succession of incidents and a closure, the cinema chain UGC reinvested in the site in 1992 and restored the complex to become the flagship of its network in Belgium.

And the magic works. What a joy to find yourself in this comfortable setting, to admire the detail of the bas-reliefs while waiting for the film to begin. An elephant's head in one corner, a jungle scene in another, it's almost like being in Africa. And what a contrast, not only with the other anonymous theatres in the De Brouckère or other cinema complex. What a pity, however, that in the programme circulated each week, the UGC management does not even mention which film has the honour of being shown in the Gran Eldorado.

For those who enjoy this exotic style of decoration, take a stroll along the banana route while in the city centre (see p. 26).

BELGIAN MUSEUM
OF FREEMASONRY

Everything you always wanted to know about
Freemasons but never dared ask

Rue de Laeken 73
02 223 06 04
Tuesday to Friday 10am–12pm (and 1pm–5pm group visits only, on
reservation), Saturday 1pm–4pm
Metro Sainte-Catherine or De Brouckère

oused in the Hôtel Dewez, a listed 18th-century building, the Belgian Museum of Freemasonry is an excellent way to learn about the historical origins of the brotherhood, the meaning of the various symbols, such as the compass and set square, and everything you always wanted to know about Freemasonry but were afraid to ask, all thanks to the exhibition of over 300 pieces dating from the 18th century to the present. If you have any questions, don't keep them to yourself! Tour guides are pleased to take groups on an initiatory journey of an hour and a half, but if you turn up on your own you'll always find someone ready to help.

Although the temples of 79 rue de Laeken are in theory open only to Masons, group visits can also be arranged on reservation: an opportunity not to be missed.

At last, for those wondering what a Freemason's final answer would be, there's the response of A. Uyttebrouck: 'Symbolically, the Freemason works on the construction of the temple of humanity, the internal temple, that is to say the progress of the individual himself, by greater knowledge of himself, and the external temple, which is the progress of humanity.'

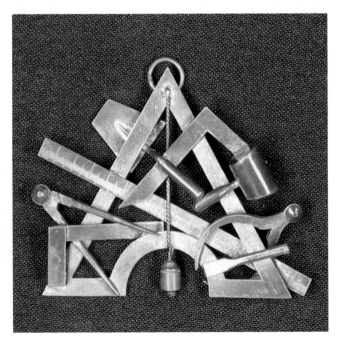

THÉÂTRE *PLAZA*

A beautiful Moorish-style room

Boulevard Adolphe Max 118–126

Simply by asking at the reception of the Plaza Hotel, it is possible to gain entry to the magnificent hotel theatre, a former cinema covering a surface area of 460 m², which has been classified as a historical monument by royal decree.

Constructed in 1930 in a unique Hispano-Arabo-Moorish style,

and an absolutely unique example of its kind, the auditorium is a little architectural gem which has preserved its boxes, its period wall lamps and its stage and wall decorations, richly sculpted in an Andalusian fashion.

NEARBY
Impasse Van Hoeter ⑭
Quai aux Foins 13–15
A fine courtyard in central Brussels. Built in 1848 par C. Van Hoeter, the lane leads to a dozen dwellings whose façades are currently being renovated following an explosion. A beautiful entrance porch.

FRUIT FROM THE GÉRARD KONINCKX FRÈRES BUILDING

Souvenirs of a banana and orange merchant

Boulevard d'Ypres 34–36

Boulevard d'Ypres 34–36 is a beautiful art deco building built in 1935 by architect E. De Boelpaepe for the company Gérard Koninckx Frères. Don't miss the beautiful inscription typical of this movement that decorates the top of the building, or the sculpted reliefs of two bunches of bananas and oranges at the top of the building's four pilasters, a reminder of Gérard Koninckx Frères' involvement in the banana and orange trade.

© Jean-Jacques Evrard

The façade has the typical layout of an establishment of this type: the first two floors are dedicated to the unloading dock and warehouses, and the four floors above are occupied by flats.

Two other Gérard Koninckx Frères buildings

Gérard Koninckx Frères owned two other buildings in the district. The first, at nos. 22 and 23 Place du Nouveau Marché aux Grains, is less interesting and was also used for a variety of purposes: banana storage in the cellar, an unloading and packing bay on the ground floor, a garage on the first floor and shops and offices on the top floors. The other, on the corner of Rue Antoine Dansaert and Rue du Vieux Marché aux Grains, is spectacular and also has a banana theme (see p. 26).

MAXIMILIAN PARK FARM

A city-centre farm among the modern buildings

Quai du Batelage 2
02 201 56 09
lafermeduparcmaximilien.be
Tuesday to Friday 10am–5pm, Saturday 12pm–4pm, closed Monday and
Sunday (reduced opening hours in low season)
Metro Yser

The farm in the Parc Maximilien is an absolutely amazing place, only a 10-minute walk from Brussels' Grand-Place. Wedged among the modern buildings in the district surrounding the Gare du Nord, the Petit Ring, and the immense Citroën garage at place de l'Yser, this urban farm is a breath of fresh air.

It also offers some highly unusual sights in the heart of a big city: a sheep peacefully grazing in the long grass alongside the farmhouse, chickens pecking at grain against the background of an Art Deco garage and a Haussmann-style building, a goat meandering by a colossal public housing block…

Once inside, go for a quiet stroll in this patch of countryside in the city centre, feed the ducks and rabbits, gather eggs, or tend the orchard and vegetable garden. Workshops are organized regularly around these activities and more generally to make visitors more aware of environmental issues. There are also events for local children and school groups.

The farm, set up entirely from scratch to replace a car park in the 1990s, is now a big hit.

At the corner of boulevard Baudouin and avenue de l'Héliport, note also three steel statues representing farm animals: a rooster, a pig and a cow. Installed in October 1999 a short distance from the entrance to the farm to indicate its presence, they are the work of Belgian artist Pierre Martens, painter, screen-printer and sculptor.

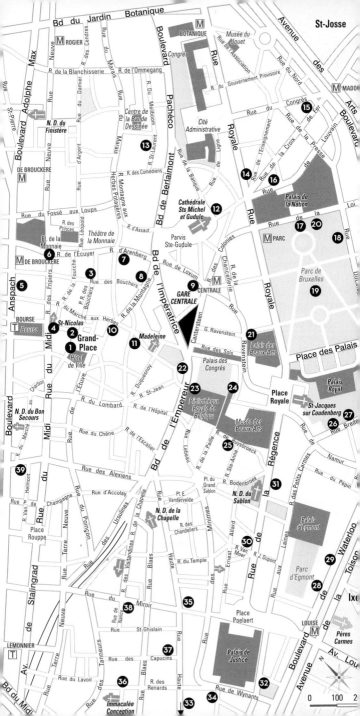

Centre East of the Boulevards

AN ALCHEMICAL INTERPRETATION ①
OF THE GRAND-PLACE

The seven operations to obtain the philosopher's stone are represented here

Metro Gare centrale

The world-famous Grand-Place of Brussels, which has been showered with so much praise and commentaries of various kinds, has also been the object of an esoteric analysis which is less well known but nevertheless interesting. Put forward by Paul de Saint-Hilaire but disputed by many other experts, this theory contends that the Grand-Place is one of the key locations for Freemasonry in Brussels. Without recapping the entire history, we simply note here that most of this site was destroyed in 1695 under the bombardment ordered by Maréchal de Villeroi, who sought to seize the city on behalf of the French monarch, Louis XIV. This is the historical starting-point on which Saint-Hilaire bases part of his Masonic interpretation of these surroundings. According to him, the reconstruction of the Grand-Place was carried out by Freemason architects who riddled their constructions with Masonic and alchemical symbols.

First of all, Saint-Hilaire sees in the superposing of the three major architectural orders (Doric, Ionic and Corinthian), frequently found in the buildings around the square, a correspondence with the three Masonic ranks of apprentice, journeyman and master. But some will no doubt reply that this succession is common in all Baroque compositions on such a colossal scale. But Saint-Hilaire pursues his explanation: according to him, seven streets lead into the Grand-Place, dividing it into seven groups of constructions, most of which are composed of seven houses, and corresponding to the seven operations required to obtain the philosopher's stone.

The first operation can be discerned in the houses numbered 39 to 34, to which should be added the seventh house, located at 46 rue au Beurre, called Notre-Dame-de-Paix. The seven houses to the north-east (No. 20 to 28) comprise the second operation. Anne and Joseph, placed under the same roof in the house at No. 22, would thus represent the preparation of the male-female alliance, symbolized by the alliance of sulphur and mercury. The Maison du Roi stands for the third operation: the two-headed eagle above the entrance would thus indicate the successful amalgamation of the male and female principles, of the King and the Queen, which was evoked in a motto inscribed on the façade in 1767 but since disappeared. The Maison du Roi leads to the famous 'Roi d'Espagne' building (No. 1 and 2) whose octagonal dome would thus represent the athanor, the furnace in which the amalgam is produced. Then the crucible must be removed from the fire with the help of a 'wheelbarrow' (No. 3), before it is isolated in a 'sack' (No. 4). Next, air is blown on the vessel by means of a special horn, the 'cornet' (No. 6), an action also symbolized by the four winds visible at the top of the ship's prow.

And alchemists also gave the name 'boat' or 'fish' to the solid matter that appears on the surface of the liquid as it congeals. The fifth operation is alluded to by part of the eastern group of buildings, the Maison des Ducs de Brabant; and the sixth by the southern group, running from No. 14 to No. 8, called L'Étoile, the alchemists' star: this shines brightly like the philosopher's stone just obtained. Lastly, the Hôtel de Ville would symbolize the seventh and final operation. According to Saint-Hilaire, the building's asymmetry can also be explained by alchemy: the first method for obtaining the philosopher's stone included twelve steps corresponding to the twelve arches of this building, whose first stones were laid in 1402. But the alchemist Nicolas Flamel, who died in 1418, invented in Santiago

de Compostela a new method requiring only seven steps, the 'short' or 'dry' way, represented by the seven arches of the right wing, added later. For those who would like to learn more, see the guidebook *Bruxelles Mystérieux* by Paul de Saint-Hilaire (now out of print, but still to be found second-hand in some bookshops), or else the brochure *Itinéraire de la franc-maçonnerie à Bruxelles*, published by the Société Royale Belge de Géographie.

For more information about alchemy, see the following double page.

Alchemy

Most religious orders of the Middle Ages and the Renaissance considered alchemy (from the Coptic term *Allah-Chemia*, or divine chemistry) as the *Art of the Holy Spirit* or *Royal Art* of the divine creation of the world and man. It was connected to Orthodox Catholic doctrine.

The followers of this art divided it into two principal forms.

Spiritual alchemy exclusively concerns the inspiration of the soul, transforming the impure elements of the body in the refined states of spiritual consciousness, which is also called the *Way of the Repentants*. *Laboratory alchemy*, called the *Way of the Philosophers*, reproduces the alchemical universe of the transmutation of nature's impure elements into noble metals, such as silver and gold, in the laboratory. These two alchemical practices are generally followed in combination, thus becoming the *Way of the Humble*, where the humility is that of man faced with the

grandeur of the universe reproduced in the laboratory (in Latin *labor* + *oratorium*); the alchemy of the (interior) soul is expressed exteriorly in the laboratory.

Those who practise *Laboratory alchemy* with the sole purpose of finding silver and gold, and thus neglect the essential aspects of the betterment of the soul, will fail and become charlatans, who might have a wide-ranging culture but certainly not the required moral qualities.

To avoid becoming a *charlatan* (it was this heretic form that was condemned by the Church), followers must balance the heart and soul, culture and moral qualities, penitence and humility, to become a true philosopher.

The 12 steps of the alchemical great work and their symbols

The alchemical Great Work can be expressed as a series of laboratory operations on the substance of the chemical elements of Nature, eliminating their physical impurities (Death), purifying and reuniting them (Resurrection), with mercury and sulphur (Soul and Spirit) acting on salt (base matter). Thus the volatile elements fixed in purified matter will gradually, over the 12 steps, create the philosopher's stone, which is synonymous with the Illumination of Matter by the release of the Spirit imprisoned within it.

These 12 interconnected steps are briefly outlined here for those who may be unfamiliar with hermetic thought and language. They are carried out in three distinct stages, each divided into four steps.

Nigredo (blackness) – dissolution and putrefaction of matter

Calcination – this is the purification of the original solid matter by fire, without decreasing its water content (referred to as 'Dew'), so that it chars without turning to ashes. Its symbol is the *lion*, which indicates strength and solar light, as shown in alchemical iconography by the operator who maintains the balance of fire and water. This step is also symbolised by the *dragon* in flames.

Solution or Dissolution – the solid matter is transformed, reduced to the liquid state and dispersed in this solvent: the "philosophical dissolution" where the water is mercury itself, which dissolves the essence of the differentiated chemical element by integrating it with its undifferentiated original state, the raw material. The

symbol of this step is a *crowned man* (follower of the 'royal art') *bathing in a lake* (the 'mercurial waters') and expresses an internal leap of faith.

Separation – just as the Spirit is distinct from the Soul, mercury is separated from its sulphur component, and when heated to the correct temperature coagulates by a secret process (*Secretum Secretorum*) only known to alchemists. This is a form of dividing line between alchemy and chemistry, metaphorically capturing a sunray inside a glass flask (or 'philosophical egg'), condensing it and hermetically sealing it by heating the flask on the fire.

The Earth – the solid element – remains at the bottom, while the Spirit rises. Once this step is successfully completed, a star (the 'rainbow' or 'peacock's tail') can be seen forming in the flask. This stage is marked in alchemical iconography by the *shining star*, also by the *knight's sword*.

Putrefaction – heat kills the solid bodies in the flask and they decay: a dark blackish colour then forms, represented by two *crows* (one indicating calcination and the other putrefaction), or by the *Grim Reaper* with his scythe, and sometimes by a Moor or simply a *decapitated and blackened head*.

Albedo (whiteness) – purification of matter by the 'liquid' substance

Conjunction – aware of their separate existence, the Soul and the Spirit, mercury and sulphur, are reunited. This operation is carried out in the same tightly sealed flask. Because this step represents the 'hermetic wedding', it is symbolised by a *King* (Spirit, Sun) and a *Queen* (Soul, Moon) with their hands clasped together.

Coagulation or Congelation – in this step, an off-white colour appears in the flask, gently heated to cause the change in the matter. This is the cooling process which solidifies a liquid: the previously dissolved solid reappears and the solvent evaporates. It signifies the return of the duly cleansed element to the Earth, as in the resurrection of the body, and is represented by a *King bearing a sceptre rising from his tomb*.

Cibation – this step is the addition of the chemical elements needed to feed the dry matter in the crucible, represented by a dragon framed by the Sun and Moon.

Sublimation – in this step, matter becomes spiritual and mind becomes matter, i.e. what is fixed evaporates and what is volatile is fixed, but these two processes are interdependent, otherwise it is impossible to vaporise (disappear) or fix (solidify). The predominant role is once again that of the element Air, the principle of sublimation of the Spirit and of Matter, because this is where vapour solidifies and dry matter rises on the application of heat. This step is said to last 40 days. The symbolic iconography may equally well show a *dove descending into the crucible* or an *eagle rising from the crucible*. Other representations are that of an *old man lying prone* with a dove hovering over him and an eagle perched on his stomach, while above him are the astrological symbols of the seven classical planets (Sun, Moon, Mars, Mercury, Jupiter, Venus, Saturn).

Rubedo (redness) – when the philosopher's stone is created

Fermentation – this is the reaction of an organic body to matter that causes it to decompose, as well as the chemical transformation accompanied by natural effervescence from fermentation or a similar process. However, in alchemy it was customary to add gold to activate the reaction, given that 'Nature reproduces from Nature herself'. The symbols of fermentation are images of the *hermaphrodite* and the *wine barrel*, sometimes replaced by the figure of the god *Bacchus* or *Dionysus*.

Exaltation – this step is identical to sublimation, a kind of resublimation or spiritual exaltation which is at the same time chemical, marked by the presence of gold and mercury. It is indicated by images of the *god Jupiter with his arrows of fire and the mermaid Melusine* signifying the 'mercury of the philosophers'.

Multiplication – in this step, further heating the matter increases its power without increasing its quantity. This matter becomes the 'powder of projection' required for the transmutation of base metals into pure gold. This is when the philosopher's stone starts to appear in its primitive form.

The Bible describes this process of multiplication in Christ's Miracle of the Loaves, and the iconic allegories are the lake and its waters of 'eternal youth' and a *goat standing on a mount*.

Projection – this is the final application of the philosopher's stone as it was habitually employed, such as in the transmutation of base metal, by throwing the stone or its 'powder of projection' onto the molten metal to turn it into gold. Given a bright red or purple colouring, the philosopher's stone – issue of the sublimated salt which is the quintessence of matter – is represented by a *crowned Child*. Descendant of the King and Queen, the Sun and the Moon, sulphur and mercury, he is the divine Crown Prince, dressed sometimes in immaculate white, sometimes in luminous purple. He represents the revelation of Spirit over Matter, and therefore the illumination of the body by the Divine Essence, the ultimate goal of true alchemists.

This step is also represented by the *hedgehog* and the sacred *chalice* that the knights of old on their spiritual quest named the *Holy Grail*.

THE CAPITALS
OF THE TOWN HALL

Medieval rebuses carved in the stone

Grand-Place
Metro Gare centrale

The statues that ornament the façade of the town hall hide their secrets well. Indeed, beneath the somewhat austere look of the roughly 300 sculptures, which appear medieval but are entirely neo-Gothic (they were placed in the various niches around 1850), authentic medieval rebuses are hidden in the capitals, keystones and *cul-de-lampes* (pendent ornaments) of the right-wing gallery. They provide the names of the houses that once stood here before they were demolished during the construction of the right wing of the town hall around 1440.

In memory of these ancestral buildings, the sculptors ornamented the capitals with entertaining scenes. Starting from the left, in the first scene the characters joyously stack up chairs using large shovels. By combining the Flemish words for chair *(stoel)* and shovel *(scup)*, you get the word *scupstoel*, which means *strappado*, a cruel form of torture reserved for condemned prisoners that led to their death. This depiction is a reminder of the fact that the Grand-Place was the site of executions for many years, as the prisoner's sentence was carried out directly opposite the town hall's courtroom.

In a lighter vein, the centre capital shows monks holding beers in their hands and enjoying a feast in a cellar. The house bore the name of *papenkelder*, or monks' cave. The last and most complex one depicts, on the right, a Moorish scene where lovers kiss in a harem, while, on the left, a mother nurses her baby next to a cradle. The house was called De Moer, but it seems that when the town hall was built, they had already forgotten the origin of this name: was it in reference to the Moors or was it a distortion of the word Moeder, meaning mother? Preferring to compromise, the artists carved both possibilities in the stone.

CERAMICS AT RESTAURANT
CHEZ VINCENT

The only interior in the Brussels region with entirely tiled ceilings and walls

Rue des Dominicains 8–10
02 511 26 07 or 02 511 23 03
Daily 12pm–2.45pm and 6.30pm–11.30pm (10.30pm Sunday)

Admire the façade and above all the remarkable interior decor with ceramics from the Société Helman, dating from 1913. It is the only interior in the Brussels region where the ceilings and walls are

entirely tiled, with illustrations of fishing scenes and rural landscapes. The traditional fare is rather good.

NEARBY
Cannonball of Saint Nicholas Church ④
Rue de Tabora

Well-known to Brussels residents, especially for the picturesque little houses adjoining its south-eastern façade, the Saint-Nicolas church has a surprising memento from the bombardment of the city by the Maréchal de Villeroi en 1695: upon entering the nave, you can see a cannonball embedded at a height of about 3 m in the fifth pillar on the left.

THE FORMER 'LA GRANDE MAISON DE BLANC' SHOP

Magnificent art nouveau ceramics by Privat-Livemont

Rue du Marché aux Poulets 32–34

The former La Grande Maison de Blanc shop is an important example of art nouveau ceramics in Belgium. It was founded in 1894 by E. Lefebre and it was there that the Brussels bourgeoisie bought their 'blanc', i.e. lingerie, hosiery and clothing.

The current building was built in 1896–1897, according to plans by architect Oscar François. The monumental appearance of the building, which reflected the scale of the business at the time, did not stand up to the ravages of time. It gradually lost its original purpose and was successively transformed into a supermarket, a hotel and then an amusement arcade. Along with its transformations, its façade was gradually disfigured.

Between 2000 and 2007, the building was restored to its former glory, in particular the remarkable art nouveau-style ceramics produced by the Boch faience factory in La Louvière according to designs by Henri Privat-Livemont (1861–1936).

The impressive second floor features ceramics depicting the allegory of trade and industry and a series of women in a beautiful floral design typical of art nouveau. On the third floor, the ceramic panels depict magnificent, stylised flowers.

Although it has been badly damaged, the first floor still features a few rare remnants of its original decor. The ground floor, however, bears no resemblance to its original layout.

© EmDee

THE SECRETS OF THE OPÉRA ROYAL DE LA MONNAIE

From the foyer to the workshops,
La Monnaie is revealed

Place de la Monnaie
lamonnaiedemunt.be
Guided tour one Saturday a month (see dates, times and practical information
on the website)
Metro De Brouckère

The guided tour of the Opéra Royal de la Monnaie invites visitors to slip behind the curtain to discover the magical world of this theatre whose walls have echoed with the most famous voices for over 300 years. From the moment the tour begins in the foyer, you are welcomed in a sumptuous, exquisite and elegant ambiance. Two majestic staircases guarded by a series of cherubs descend into this vast foyer, where the dominant theme is contemporary plastic design. Since the 1980s, the ceiling has been decorated with an immense Sam Francis painting, a triptych animated with moving organic forms in bright colours. In contrast, the floor is paved with a rigorous black-and-white geometric pattern designed by Sol LeWitt.

From the foyer, you head to the grand auditorium covered in gilded *trompe-l'œil* paintings and cherubs. The decor was orchestrated by Joseph Poelaert, the architect of the law courts, who was chosen to rebuild the theatre after a fire almost destroyed it entirely in 1855. True to his inimitable style and taste for the prolific, he enhanced the auditorium with a number of symbols related to Belgium's recently won independence, such as the initials SPQB (*Senatus Populus Que Bruxellensis*), the monogram of Leopold II, and the large fresco that decorates the ceiling in which there is an allegory of Belgium protecting the arts.

The opera boxes that line the auditorium, so neatly draped with cardinal red curtains, did not always look like this. In fact, noble families used to hire them by the year, so each box was decorated according to the tastes of its occupant. You'll have to imagine them adorned in the fashionable colours of the 18th and 19th centuries. As for the respectful silence that welcomes the performers today, that custom dates from the early 20th century. Before, audience members would call out to one another and chat throughout the performance, leaving and entering the auditorium to warm themselves in the Grand Foyer, the only heated area of the theatre. La Monnaie is also composed of the plethora of artistic trades involved in producing an opera: seamstresses, architects, hatters, wigmakers, cobblers, sculptors, carpenters and the others who, day after day, create and build the dreams and magic that turn the opera into a magnificent and legendary universe.

The originality of this guided tour lies precisely in the fact that visitors step through the doors and enter this universe that is so often kept secret.

Once the curtain has been raised to reveal the reality of the opera house, the only thing left to do is to go along on the night of a performance to share a unique experience of the performing arts.

CINÉMA NOVA

This alternative cinema in rough concrete is a little gem of underground architecture

Rue d'Arenberg 3
02 511 24 77
nova-cinema.com
Metro Gare centrale

Three minutes on foot from the Grand-Place, the Nova is probably the most atypical cinema in Brussels, and not to be missed. Seeing a movie in the quasi-industrial decor of its theatre is a real and somewhat disorienting pleasure.

Installed in a building constructed at the end of the 19th century, the present theatre was previously home to a cabaret, a vaudeville show, and finally in the 1930s an art house cinema, the Studio Arenberg. After several overhauls, the latter finally closed its doors in May 1987 and the space was used for furniture storage.

Ten years later, in January 1997, the Nova association took over the place to recreate an alternative cinema. Today it is a little gem of underground architecture, without carpets or velvet, without any old-fashioned decorations or trimmings, but instead plenty of rough concrete. And that's its charm.

The programming is devoted exclusively to independent films and videos. Between experimental films, shorts and features by obscure Lithuanian directors, it also hosts some small specialized festivals, including a horror film festival of some renown held every year around March.

Finally, don't forget to have a drink in the basement, still in the same post-modern style, where exhibitions, concerts, and other artistic activities regularly take place.

NEARBY

Résidence Centrale   ⑧

Rue de la Montagne 52

At No. 52 rue de la Montagne, which has rather suffered from the construction of soulless hotels, a little jewel of tranquility is concealed. When you step through the entrance (generally left open), you find yourself in a courtyard enlivened by the soft gurgling of water. The buildings surrounding it were built in 1943 following a modernist aesthetic found in the designs of the architect, Linssen. Above one of the basins, a bronze fountain from 1953 that has taken on a pretty patina, a young, innocent girl is shown in a crouching position. This delicate and deliciously suggestive statue is the work of Romanian artist Idel Ianchelevici.

ROYAL LODGE
IN THE GARE CENTRALE

*A place for the royal family to wait for their train
in conditions reflecting their rank*

Gare Centrale
02 224 50 40
Visits by appointment
Metro Gare Centrale

O n leaving Galerie Ravenstein, anyone using the pedestrian crossing over rue Cantersteen will notice that this crossing does not lead directly to the entrance of the Gare Centrale (Central Station) but to

a door covered by a shutter. Above this door with its beautiful black marble surround, the Belgian royal coat of arms and its motto 'L'union fait la force' (Unity makes strength) act as a reminder that this is the entrance to the Royal Lodge of the Gare Centrale: here the royal family could wait for the train in conditions reflecting their rank. Although the lodge is no longer used by the royals, it is still used occasionally by the SNCB (National Railway Company of Belgium) for prestigious events. In fact, members of the royal family were able to reach the Gare Centrale on foot from Place Royale via Galerie Ravenstein. Ironically, during the opening of the Gare Centrale, King Baudouin arrived by limousine at the Royal Lodge and then made the short journey to Bruxelles-Midi (Brussels South) Station, which was also provided with a Royal Lodge.

The interior of the lodge, as well as the stairway and elevator leading to it, are richly decorated. There are large amounts of gilding, white marble walls, leather armchairs from the Delvaux workshops designed by Henry van de Velde, toilets with golden taps and a beautiful (broken) clock. The Royal Lodge was used intensively during the Universal Exhibition of 1958. The Belgian Royal Family received (among others) the Thai royal couple, the Negus of Ethiopia and the Shah of Iran there. Inside the station, at the foot of the large stairway leading to the waiting hall, another door (also covered with a shutter, surrounded by black marble and bearing the royal coat of arms) indicates the other entrance to the Royal Lodge. This is open to the general public on heritage days or upon request to the SNCB.

NEARBY

Plaque at Rue du Marché-aux-Herbes 85 ⑩

Thousands of tourists regularly pass by this plaque, a short distance from the Grand-Place, without noticing it. But it announces an important piece of patriotic information. It was here on 26 August 1830 that Madame Abts sewed the first two Belgian flags.

FAÇADE OF THE MARJOLAINE SHOP

A fine example of Art Nouveau architecture

Rue de la Madeleine 7

J ust a stone's throw from the Grand Place, Marjolaine is one of the last remaining Art Nouveau shopfronts in Brussels (see opposite). Despite its central location, many Brussels residents, not to mention tourists, are strangely unaware of this little architectural gem.

The shop's magnificent façade was designed by the architect Léon Sneyers in 1904, in a geometric Art Nouveau style.

The circular stained-glass window separating the shop window from

© EmDee

the entrance door is heavily influenced by the Viennese Secession style. The windows were restored in 1996 by Jean-Marc Gdalewitch.

Other Art Nouveau shop fronts in Brussels

Chemiserie Niguet (Paul Hankar, 1896 – see p. 70)
Falstaff Tavern (next to the Stock Exchange – E. Houbion, 1903)
Pharmacie du Bon Secours (boulevard Anspach 160 – Paul Hamesse, 1910)

THE LEGEND OF THE STAINED GLASS IN THE CATHEDRAL OF ST. MICHAEL AND ST. GUDULA

An anti-Semitic legend

Cathédrale Saints-Michel-et-Gudule
Place Sainte-Gudule
Metro Gare centrale

At the end of the right nave of the Cathedral of St. Michael and St. Gudula, 15 beautiful stained glass windows recount a legend dating from the 14th century that was hostile to the Jewish community of Brussels. It has subsequently been shown that this story was an anti-Semitic fabrication. A plaque to that effect was installed in the 1970s in the Chapel of the Blessed Sacrament (Saint-Sacrement).

Window 1: a banker called Jonathas asks Jean de Louvain to steal some communion wafers (hosts) for him in exchange for sixty gold coins (*moutons d'or*).

Window 2: Jonathas pays Jean and mocks the hosts in front of his friends.

Window 3: In retaliation, Jonathas is killed in his garden in front of his horrified son.

Window 4: Jonathas' widow and son take refuge among the Jews of Brussels and give the hosts to them.

Window 5: The Jews gathered in the synagogue place the hosts on a table and stab them: blood flows miraculously from the wafers.

Window 6: Wanting to rid themselves of the hosts, the worried Jews entrust Catherine with giving them to the Jews of Cologne.

Window 7: Instead of going to Cologne, Catherine visits her parish priest.

Window 8: Catherine is questioned by the Duke and Duchess of Brabant.

Window 9: The Jews admit their crime, and are consequently condemned to be burned at the stake.

Window 10: The Bishop of Cambrai must settle a dispute between the Church of Notre-Dame-De-La-Chapelle and the cathedral as they both lay claim to the hosts.

Window 11: A young weaver sees a ray of light coming from the tabernacle containing the hosts.

Window 12: Margaret of Austria organises the Procession of the Blessed Sacrament to celebrate the miraculous hosts.

Window 13: During the Wars of Religion, the authorities fear that the hosts will be destroyed and decide to hide them.

Window 14: The decision is made to hide the hosts once again, this time in the beam of a house. Once peace has finally been restored, the archbishop himself comes to remove them from the beam. This fragment of the beam is subsequently kept in the Chapel of the Blessed Sacrament, where it may still be found today.

Window 15: The cardinal officially 'reinstates' the Blessed Sacrament, offering a document to the parish priest of the church.

'SO THAT THE PEOPLE CAN READ' INSCRIPTION

A reminder of the fight against illiteracy

Le Peuple former printing works
Rue Saint-Laurent 28

On the façade of the building at no. 28 rue Saint-Laurent, on either side of the entrance, is a bas-relief by Dolf Ledel with a large inscription: 'Pour que le peuple lise' ('So that the people can read').

This phrase was coined by Joseph Wauters, a Belgian politician who died in 1929. He was always at the forefront of the fight against illiteracy and promoted compulsory schooling. Elected as a Member of Parliament in 1908, he became Minister for Industry, Labour and Supply in 1918 and in 1921 passed the law on the 8-hour working day and the 48-hour working week. He was also the man behind the creation of unemployment insurance and the first old-age pensions.

In 1910, he headed the socialist newspaper *Le Peuple*, that had been founded in 1885 and whose offices and printing works were built here in 1931-1932 by the architects Fernand and Maxime Brunfaut.

Designed in a modernist liner style strongly influenced by Russian Constructivism, the building is characterised by its use of light and transparency thanks to its large bay windows and polygonal tower.

The high part of the adjoining wall, which still bears the newspaper's sign, rises like a banner above the neighbouring roofs.

For many years, the building was abandoned but has been listed since April 1989. It was restored from top to bottom in June 2003 and since 2015, it has been home to the PIAS (for Play It Again, Sam) record label. The building welcomes a concert hall, a restaurant and a vinyl and CD shop packed with unreleased treasures.

FORMER NIGUET SHIRT SHOP

Art Nouveau temple to the florist's art

Rue Royale 13
Monday to Friday 9am–6.30pm, Saturday 9am–2pm
Metro Parc

Long neglected, deteriorating little by little with each passing tenant, and finally abandoned, the former gents' outfitters 'Niguet' has just emerged from three years and 11 months of restoration work.

Today the premises are the showcase for florist Daniel Ost. He should be thanked for having matched form and function so well: what could be better than a florist in this finest flower of Art Nouveau? Prior to his arrival, curious passers-by had to content themselves with

admiring the magnificent façade. It's impossible not be fascinated by the extravagant curls and whirling knots of wood that nevertheless remain remarkably well-restrained in size and rhythmic distribution around the display window.

The building at 13 rue Royale was one of the first projects undertaken by Paul Hankar (1859–1901) and was very popular when it was inaugurated in 1896.

The curving forms, although typically Art Nouveau, are somewhat surprising from this architect who tended to favour more geometric variants of this style. The shop's interior decor is more characteristic of his work, with the magnificent murals by Adolphe Crespin (his habitual partner) and the windmill-sail pattern he tended to favour.

But be sure to see it during opening hours – once closed, the shop's shutter hides the woodwork.

© Fred Romero from Paris, France

ICEHOUSES AT PLACE SURLET-DE-CHOKIER

Hooks where the butchers stored their meat

Place Surlet de Chokier 15–17
Accessible on heritage days or on request by telephoning 02 801 72 11
Metro Madou

O n heritage days, or on request to the Government of the Wallonia-Brussels Federation which occupies the premises (see telephone number on opposite page), it is possible to visit the little-known and astonishing icehouses at place Surlet-de-Chokier.

These two large halls, which are reached by a small, narrow stairway, were rediscovered in 1989 by pure chance during the construction of the building for the Government of the Wallonia-Brussels Federation. While carrying out excavation work under the building for a new car park, the workers discovered this immense icehouse measuring 19,000 m³. The hooks used by butchers for storing their meat allowed historians to determine the previous function of this space.

Since the Bronze Age, mankind has looked for methods of preserving ice accumulated during the winter months, by storing it in underground cavities, caves, wells or ice cellars. Icehouses became more common in the 17th and 18th centuries, not only for preserving foodstuffs and beer production but also for medicinal and industrial uses. Indeed, many stately homes and estates had their own icehouses.

In the cities, large communal icehouses were constructed. In winter, the natural ice was cut out of nearby ponds or transported by boat from colder regions.

Thus, in 19th-century Brussels, there were more than 30 active ice companies. Around 1860, the arrival of the steam engine made new artificial ice-production techniques possible, which brought this trade to a halt shortly before the First World War. Initially, the icehouses continued to be used as a storage facility for artificially produced ice, but eventually they became redundant and fell into obscurity.

NEARBY

Van Damme Pharmacy

Rue de Louvain 22
Monday to Friday 8.30am–2pm and 3pm–6pm
A very beautiful pharmacy, built in 1826 and renovated in 1876 following a fire, with attractive period furnishings.

COMMEMORATION OF TSAR PETER THE GREAT'S VOMIT

As he sat on the edge of this fountain, he ennobled its waters with the wine of his libations...

Pits of Brussels Park
Metro Parc

In the Parc Royal, opposite the palace, two strange 8 m deep pits can be seen on either side of the main path. Head towards the one on the left, but keep an eye on your virtue and your wallet, as it is often a site of debauchery, despite the presence of a sculpture of Mary Magdalene repenting in a rock grotto.

This pit, like its twin, is a vestige of the old park belonging to the castle of the Dukes of Burgundy. The castle, parts of which are still visible in the underground sections of Place Royale, was destroyed in a fire in 1731. In the late 18th century, its former park, called Warande, was levelled to create the current Parc Royal and the neighbourhood of the same name.

These two pits were not filled in during the renovations, as the scope of the task dissuaded the town councillors. Instead, they were converted into an English garden. In 1717, this site witnessed a strange spectacle.

While Peter the Great was visiting the region, he quite simply vomited here. A bronze statue given to the city by Prince Demidoff in 1856 serves as a reminder of this incredible scene, while just a few metres away a small blue stone basin surrounds the site of the incident and narrates the adventure in dog Latin along its edge: '…Insidens marcini huius fontis aquam illius nobilitavit libato vino…' ('As he sat on the edge of this fountain, he ennobled its waters with the wine of his libations').

THE PARC ROYAL BUNKER

A secret bunker 12 m underground in the Parc Royal

Accessible on request by contacting Brussels city property department:
02 279 40 45
Metro Parc

In the very heart of Brussels, underneath the Parc Royal, lies a disused bunker that has lain forgotten for many years. On the surface, around the Vauxhall building behind the Royal Park theatre, there are several features indicating the existence of this universally forgotten place: air vents, a chimney and, in the cellars of the Parliament, entrance doors for the corridors (walled up since the construction of the metro and destruction of the corridors).

Built in the utmost secrecy in 1938, 12 m underground, the Parc Royal bunker was, unlike the large shelters earmarked for the general population during the Second World War, reserved exclusively for Members of Parliament and the government. It was also intended to be used for organising aerial defence in the event of any bombing. Completely secret, it could be accessed from above ground in the Parc Royal via the cellars of the Cercle Gaulois club or directly from Parliament through two tunnels, one for the Chamber and the other for the Senate. In the event of an attack, the plan was to evacuate the political elite to the Congo from this bunker of over 700 m². All Members of Parliament were equipped with a gas mask under their desk: this was to be used if an attack took place, before moving through the corridor and sheltering in the bunker. Although there are also stories of a third tunnel leading under Parc Royal and surfacing at the Royal Palace, this has never actually been proved.

On 10 May 1939, at the outbreak of war, neither the masks nor the bunker were used, and the members of Parliament preferred to go to the Hotel Metropole, which was better lit and more comfortable than an austere bunker. After the war, the bunker was renovated for use as a fall-out shelter that could be used to activate sirens across the country in the event of a nuclear attack.

SECRET PLAN
OF BRUSSELS PARK

A freemason park?

Metro Parc

© Michel Wal

Designed by Joachim Zinner, royal gardener, and by Guimard in 1776–77, Brussels Park was conceived according to the aesthetic rules for French-style neoclassical gardens, with a plan based on perfect symmetry.

But the historian Paul de Saint-Hilaire finds more than simple symmetry at work here. He claims that, 'for those with eyes to see', the plans were drawn up according to very precise esoteric principles derived from Freemasonry. Although his arguments should be examined carefully, they nevertheless constitute an interesting theory.

The shape of the park, the alignment of the paths, and the positioning of the ponds are said to form various Masonic symbols: the compasses, set square, chisel, mallet, hammer, perpendicular, level, ruler and trowel (see diagrams on following double page).

This 'secret' plan, in Saint-Hilaire's view, is visible on one of the sculptures in the park: a few metres from the circular basin, at the crossing with the second transversal row, there are two statues on plinths by Godecharle. On the right, one of the two children symbolizing Art is holding in its hand a medallion on which is engraved this very same plan of the park.

NEARBY
The V.I.T.R.I.O.L. inscription (20)

On the embankment wall, a strange inscription in metallic lettering – L.O.I.R.T.I.V. – mirrors the inscription of the pit on the right, which reads V.I.T.R.I.O.L. These letters are the abbreviation of *Visita Interioræ Terræ Rectificando Invenies Occultum Lapidem*, which translated literally means: 'Visit the interior of the earth and in rectifying it you will find the hidden stone'. This inscription is found in the decor of the 'chambers of reflection' through which a future Masonic initiate passes before being led to the temple. The motto should thus be understood as follows: 'Descend into the depths of the earth, and in distilling you will find the stone'. These metallic letters were placed here a few years ago by an artist who undoubtedly wanted to reinforce the Masonic nature of the park, as explained above.

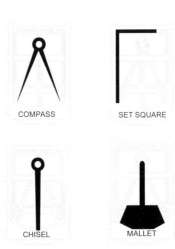

COMPASS

SET SQUARE

CHISEL

MALLET

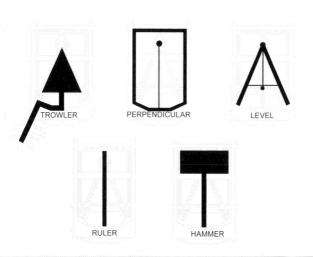

TROWLER

PERPENDICULAR

LEVEL

RULER

HAMMER

ROYAL CANOPY OF THE PALAIS DES BEAUX-ARTS

A canopy on rails, for protecting the royal family from bad weather

Rue Ravenstein 23
Metro Gare centrale

Many Brussels residents are familiar with the *Palais des Beaux-Arts* (Centre for Fine Arts): its art deco architecture (dating from 1928), its magnificent Henry Le Bœuf Hall and its annual Queen Elisabeth musical competition. However, very few people know that the architect, who was none other than Victor Horta, wished to express his thanks to Queen Elisabeth for her unconditional support in building this temple of Brussels culture. He did so in a very particular way: by giving the Centre of Fine Arts a royal entrance that is distinct from the main entrance located where the building meets the corner of rue Baron-Horta and rue Ravenstein.

The royal entrance is situated at the far right-hand of the building, as seen from rue Ravenstein, and is decorated with multicoloured stained glass. This entrance is reserved for members of the Belgian royal family: it provides access to a private lounge, where the royals can wait before entering the royal box in the great Henry Le Bœuf Hall. In order to avoid any contact between the royal family and the rest of the public, the area separating the royal lounge from the royal box is even equipped with hinged panels: this creates a private corridor, for use when the royal family is passing through.

As the finishing touch, the royal entrance on rue Ravenstein is equipped with a canopy that is usually hidden in the façade of the Centre of Fine Arts. On evenings when members of the royal family are present, however, the canopy moves forward on rails in order to protect the monarchs from any inclement weather that might surprise them between their leaving the car and entering the building. This folding canopy is therefore not used under normal circumstances although its green frame can clearly be seen set into the façade, as well as the rails installed in the pavement.

For more information about Victor Horta, see the following double page.

Victor Horta (Ghent, 1861 – Brussels, 1947)

Now a major reference internationally, Victor Horta's architecture is characterized chiefly by his use of space, light and air, all of which was revolutionary for the time. His notion of space encompassed the stairway, which was no longer limited to being an enclosed cage. His lighting flooded this space both horizontally from the windows and vertically from skylights. The quality of air in his buildings was improved by his new, particular concern with ventilation. Yet Horta was at first better known for his new forms, curves, the decorative aspects of his work, and his famous *coup de fouet* (whiplash) style.

Horta was also the first major architect to make massive use of steel in the façades of private homes. The slenderness of the metal columns took up relatively little space and allowed more light to enter. Similarly, the steel beams employed as load-bearing elements liberated more interior space. This was a risky and innovative choice at a time when steel was reserved for industrial and commercial buildings.

But his collaboration with his teacher, A. Balat, in the construction of the remarkable royal greenhouses at Laeken, had familiarized him with this material.

In his constant concern with light, Horta also made intensive use of glass, particularly stained glass.

Attracting his clientele from among the well-off, enlightened members of the Belgian bourgeoisie, Horta had considerable funds at his disposal and could thus employ high-quality materials in his work, notably bronze and marble. He also devised original models of hinges, doorknobs, keys and window catches for each house.

All his projects were integral, ground-breaking works of art that were frequently copied but never truly equalled. For the most part, his imitators' efforts were limited to the façade, sometimes with very successful results, but tending to fall back on more traditional designs for the interiors.

Buildings by Horta mentioned in this guidebook include: 6, rue Paul-Emile Janson; 224 and 346, avenue Louise (Ixelles); 37, rue Lebeau (Centre); 2, 3 and 4, avenue Palmerston (Quartier de l'Europe); 66, rue de l'Hôtel des Monnaies (Saint-Gilles); 266, chaussée de Haecht (Schaerbeek); and 80, avenue Brugmann (Forest).

UNDERGROUND FRESCOS BY DELVAUX AND MAGRITTE

The forgotten frescos by Magritte

Mont des arts
Metro Gare centrale

In the basement of the Palais des Congrès, there are two monumental frescos by the painters Paul Delvaux and René Magritte that are relatively unknown even to the inhabitants of Brussels.

The two illustrious representatives of Belgian surrealism created these frescos in 1959 and 1961 at the request of the Department of Public Education. It is said that Magritte was not particularly pleased at being allocated a smaller and less favourably situated wall than his colleague Delvaux.

In *Les Barricades mystérieuses* (Mysterious Barricades), Magritte uses elements that can be found in a number of his works: leaves, trees, a horse rider and the play of light. For his part, Delvaux, in *Le Paradis terrestre* (Paradise on Earth), depicts female figures in a scene extending over more than 40 m, reminiscent of antiquity. Both works were restored during the complete renovation of the Palais des Congrès in 2009.

NEARBY
The panoramic view from the cafeteria   ㉓
of the Royal Library
5th floor/Mont des Arts
Monday to Friday, 9am–4.15pm, except public holidays and the last week of August
Metro Gare Centrale

Although many spend time here frenetically doing research, few admire the fabulous view of Brussels from the large bay windows of the 5th-floor cafeteria. The food is not great, and neither is the coffee, but the panoramic view is worth the trip. You don't need a library card to get in, simply take one of the elevators to the 5th floor. Given the location, it's unsurprising to find such tranquility.

CHALCOGRAPHY – ROYAL LIBRARY OF BELGIUM

A superb selection of prints by the best Belgian artists

Mont des arts 28
Chalcography@kbr.be – kbr.be
By appointment only, Monday to Friday
A selection of around one hundred prints is available every day at the entrance to the KBR between 9 a.m. and 5 p.m., except on public holidays
Metro Gare centrale

The *Chalcographie de Bruxelles* is one of four places in the world, along with similar establishments in Paris, Madrid and Rome, to preserve, acquire and distribute artistic plates for printmaking. This institution, set up in 1930 following an exhibition organized by the three other chalcographic centres in 1928, is a truly special place.

Today, the Chalcographie offers prints for sale at prices that are set deliberately low in order to encourage the widest possible circulation of this art form among the general public, with considerable success.

Take a moment to browse through the numerous binders with examples of the prints available. Between Teniers, Evenepoel and Rassenfosse alone, you have a superb sample of the best Belgian artists. For a very reasonable price, ranging from €20 to €60, depending on the size of the engraving, the artist or the signature, you can bring home a print of an artist exhibited in the Musée des Beaux-Arts, just a short walk up the street.

The word 'chalcography' is derived from writing (*graphos* in Greek) on copper (*khalkos* in Greek). Today, it tends to include printing from any inscribed plate, usually but not always made from copper. The term 'engraving' has become the generic term for printing on paper from such a plate. This may be made from stone, in which case the process is called *lithography* (*lithos* being Greek for stone) or fabric, a process known as serigraphy. But neither lithography nor serigraphy are represented here. Most of the plates owned by *La Chalcographie de Bruxelles* are made from either copper or wood, the latter being an older technique that gives a more diffuse, less defined appearance to the print. Other terms are used to refer to the different techniques used for engraving the metal plate. An *eau forte* (etching), for example, is an engraving that is not inscribed directly by the artist's hand, but by the chemical action of an acid.

The collection initially comprised 2,000 engraved plates, but due to its ongoing acquisitions policy it now has over 6,000 pieces. These include some copies, thanks to a decision taken in 1980 to copy some particularly vulnerable plates (the oldest of which dates back to 1488).

PLAQUE COMMEMORATING THE *FAUX SOIR*

A historical event of a very Brussels nature

Rue de Ruysbroeck 35
Trams 94 and 93, Petit Sablon stop

At number 35 rue de Ruysbroeck, a sign recalls a historical event of a peculiarly Brussels nature. It was in this very location (the former site of Wellens Printers) that on 9 November 1943 the Independence Front, a Belgian Resistance organisation, printed the *Faux Soir* (Fake *Soir*) newspaper that gave encouragement to the inhabitants of Brussels during the Second World War.

The newspaper had been 'occupied' by the Nazis, who used it as a propaganda vehicle. It had a print run of 300,000 and featured drawings by Hergé, who received criticism for this after the war.

Printing and distributing the Faux Soir instead of the *Soir* volé (stolen *Soir*) was no small matter. It involved writing and printing a newspaper with the same format but different content in the utmost secrecy and then distributing 50,000 copies to booksellers in the afternoon (*Le Soir* was sold in the afternoon at that time).

The typographers of the real *Le Soir* were responsible for formatting the Faux Soir. The latter was, in theory, scheduled to be published on 11 November. The date was not chosen at random but deliberately to remind the Nazi occupiers of the armistice at the end of the First World War. The date selected was, however, moved forward at the last minute by two days. A message broadcast by Radio Londres from London asked people not to buy the newspaper on 11 November in protest; and 10 November was a Wednesday, the day on which *Le Soir* was normally published as four sheets instead of two, so to publish the false paper on the same day would have doubled the workload.

The creators of the Faux Soir exploited the network used by the stolen *Le Soir* and sabotaged its distribution so that the Faux Soir would replace the real *Le Soir* without the booksellers and buyers noticing immediately. This 'thumbing of the nose' at the occupiers – who were also the targets of a quite amusing but now very dated film (the aptly named *Un soir de joie*, An Evening of Joy) – was, as you might expect, very badly received by the Nazis. The Gestapo carried out investigations and several people were arrested. Some were imprisoned, others were sent to the camps and never returned. A copy of this newspaper has been preserved and can be seen at the National Museum of the Resistance in Anderlecht.

NORWEGIAN CHALET

A wooden chalet in the heart of the Royal Quarter

Rue de Brederode 10
Metro Trône

Located just behind the Royal Palace is a remarkable wooden chalet in the heart of the Royal Quarter.

The chalet was designed in 1906 by the Norwegian architect Knudsen (thus earning it the nickname 'Viking' chalet) at the specific request of Leopold II, who had fallen in love with a building in the same style and by the same architect at the Paris Universal Exhibition of 1899. The king used the chalet as a press centre for his colonial activities. It was here that he met with journalists and investors in order to publicise the Belgian Congo – as the Congolese star that can still be seen on the façade reminds us.

The building now forms part of the Royal Trust and, after being used for a period as a museum for the dynasty prior to the removal of the collections to the nearby Bellevue Museum, it is now the offices of the King Baudouin Foundation.

It was not by chance that the chalet was located in the Royal Quarter. In this area – particularly on rues de Namur, Thérésiene, des Petites-Carmes, de la Pépinière, de Brederode and Place Royale – there were numerous buildings associated with Belgian colonial ventures: ministries, civil service offices, banks, associations, etc. A number of companies with operations in the Congo for extracting raw materials such as coal, rubber, cocoa, sugar and manufacturing cement were also located there.

NEARBY
Remains of the first wall

To the right of the chalet, the relatively unobtrusive remains of the first walls surrounding the Habsburg Palace can also be seen. Constructed in the 13th century, the first Brussels walls measured 4 km in length and had seven gates for the different highways connecting the city with the surrounding towns. During the 14th century these walls were destroyed to make way for a larger and stronger set of walls. The reason that many parts of the first wall can still be seen (unlike the second, which was completely razed with the exception of the Halle Gate) is because it was not systematically dismantled but merely destroyed where it was causing an obstruction.

THE SECRETS OF PARC D'EGMONT ㉘

Peter Pan, between a tank and an icehouse

Enter at No. 31 on Boulevard de Waterloo (the rarely used entrance)
Metro Porte de Namur

A short distance from the urban hustle and bustle and the tunnels of the inner ring, Egmont Park offers exhausted passers-by the tranquility of an English garden that perpetuates the memory of a vast noble estate. This little secret garden, stunning in itself, is home to various treasures, including a statue of the mischievous Peter Pan. Sir George Frampton sculpted this work at the request of Scottish author J. M. Barrie, who created the character in 1902. Using the original illustrations by Arthur Rackham as inspiration, the sculptor surrounded 'the boy who wouldn't grow up' with the sensible Wendy and impish Tinkerbell. Around them, mischievous-looking snails, squirrels and bunnies leap out of the bronze.

The light-footed figure of Peter Pan, perched at the top of the sculpture, seems ready to take flight. The artist, moved by the suffering inflicted on Belgium during the First World War, decided to give this work to the City of Brussels as a testament to the 'bond of friendship between the children of Great Britain and those of Belgium'.

At the edge of the park near rue du Grand Cerf, the Grote Pollepel lies hidden behind the vegetation.

In the 15th century, this large tank supplied water to all the fountains on the Grand Place. This medieval vestige was unearthed during the construction of the Galerie Ravenstein's rotunda in 1955 and rebuilt stone by stone in Egmont Park.

Another surprising vestige is the old icehouse located behind the orangery. In the form of a small hill, it has an entrance of brick and white stone near the Hilton.

This precursor of the freezer was used to store blocks of ice in the winter, which were then used to keep more perishable foods cool throughout the summer months.

VERRIÈRE HERMÈS

Contemporary art in the lap of luxury

Boulevard de Waterloo 50
02 511 20 62
Monday to Friday 10am–6.30pm, Saturday 10.30am–6.30pm
Metro Louise

No indication on the outside, but at the rear of the Hermès shop in La Toison d'Or is one of the trendiest art galleries in Brussels. On entering the shop, calmly make your way to the back giving a polite hello in reply to the various shop assistants who will no doubt greet you. You'll thus gain access to a very beautiful space laid out under a wide glass roof, devoted to contemporary art exhibitions. Used for parking until 1994, this area was added on after some major building work was carried in the adjacent Hermès boutique, which had already occupied the building for over 30 years. The Verrière didn't find its present use until January 2000, when Daniel Buren, renowned for his columns at the Palais-Royal in Paris, opened the way with some in situ paintings. Next came exhibits by Eric Duyckaert, Marine Casimir and Roman Opalka, among others. Now part of the contemporary art scene in Brussels, the Verrière Hermès only hosts exhibitions at irregular intervals. Be sure to phone before stopping by.

NEARBY
Home of Jean Baes (30)
Rue Van-Moer 12

Built in 1889 by architect Jean Baes for his personal use, this handsome
house is decorated with some pretty sgraffiti by his brother, Henri Baes.
Jean Baes is known above all as the architect of the Théâtre Flamand,
built in 1884.

Sign in rue des Six Jeunes Hommes (31)
Rue des Six Jeunes Hommes, at the corner of rue des Quatre Fils Aymon

The sign of a former tavern in this neighbourhood, it perpetuates the
memory of six young jokers seeking *zwanzes* (a Belgian word for pranks)
under the harsh rule of the Spanish Duke of Alba. Examples of their
efforts included replacing holy water in the churches with ink and
attaching old ladies attending Mass to one another with pins ... But the
pranks finally ended the day they threw a jar of soot in the face of Jean
Vargas, one of Alba's collaborators. Arrested, they were sentenced to
death and hung. Today, the tradition continues because if you examine
the sign closely, you'll see that it only includes four young men, as if
some joker had kidnapped the two others in order to upset historians,
and who can tell, perhaps one day transform this sign into that of the
four Aymon sons, of the street just around the corner.

DE SMET DE NAEYER MONUMENT ㉜

The only military vessel to have sunk in the whole of Belgian history is a training ship that sank during a storm

Place Jean-Jacobs
Metro Louise

Situated next to an urban motorway, a remarkable statue recalls a particularly tragic, albeit completely forgotten, disaster. The monument pays homage to thirty-three crew members who drowned in 1906 when the training ship *Comte de Smet de Naeyer* was shipwrecked.

It is ironic to note that it is the only military vessel in the whole of Belgian naval military history to have sunk. Moreover, it was not damaged during a battle in wartime, but sank as the result of a violent storm off the Spanish coast.

After the shipwreck, 26 crew members were rescued by a French boat. They told of how Captain Fourcault and his crew made every effort to save the vessel and its sailors. Water entered the boat but the crew, which consisted mostly of young naval cadets, were unable to find the place where the boat had been damaged. As they couldn't repair the breach, the men on board exhausted themselves operating the hand-pumps.

As a last resort, Captain Fourcault gave the order to abandon ship and man the lifeboats, but some of these capsized due to the crew members' haste in evacuating the ship. The 26 crew members who were saved were in the only lifeboat that did not capsize.

The survivors related a quite unusual anecdote: the final words of Captain Fourcault, who was the last remaining person on the ship, a cigarette in his mouth, were: 'One last cigarette before I die'. The statue is supposed to represent a young man enthused by the call of the sea whose worried mother is trying to hold him back.

A wave and debris from the ship can be seen at the foot of the statue.

ART)&(MARGES MUSEUM

At the limits of art

Rue Haute 312–314
02 533 94 90
artetmarges.be
Wednesday to Sunday, 11am–6pm
Metro Porte de Hal

This brand new museum dedicated to 'outsider' art brings together works created by the psychologically fragile, those with learning difficulties, or lone artists excluded from the professional artistic scene. Although the two-level museum is small, it feels as if it is a true abyss. Flirting with the limits of art, and thus consequently defining its conditions, and defying any established system, each work has its own necessarily unique universe that is often represented to the point of obsession. Although these works may seem unimpressive at first glance as they are made from everyday materials, they can prove to be very moving for attentive spectators, as they draw you into a unique emotional and aesthetic realm.

Take, for example, Juanma Gonzalez, a shoemaker from Boitsfort who paints tranquil landscapes on the backs of shoes he has just resoled; Georges Counasse, a baker who came late to his marvellous world of miniature carousels and fairground stalls; or Jacques Trovic, who creates enchanting embroideries and patchwork pieces using ordinary hessian fabric. Appropriately, the museum doesn't try to categorize the artists it presents and provides little information on them. On the contrary, it allows the works to present their unsettling beauty to visitors fully and directly.

NEARBY

Commemorative plaque of the symbolic burial of a developer

Rue de Montserrat, opposite No. 15

In the 1960s, the City of Brussels approved a vast project to extend the courthouse. The new administrative offices of this massive organization were planned to replace the Marolle working-class neighbourhood. The residents, informed of their expropriation by mail, were infuriated and organized their resistance, which was led by Priest Jacques Van Der Biest, a fervent defender of the destitute. This marked the beginning of the 'battle of Marolle'. For the first time in history, the residents won! The developer was driven away and his (symbolic) burial was organized. In remembrance of this victory, a plaque proudly announces 'Here lies the developer and his faithful wife, bureaucracy…burial plot held in perpetuity'.

Ceramics at Rue Haute 146

Tuesday to Saturday 12pm–2.30pm and 6.30pm–10.30pm (Sunday 12pm–2.30pm)
02 513 54 40

This trendy pizzeria warrants a brief detour to admire its two superb ceramic panels, created by R. Inghelbrecht in 1918. One represents the making of cakes and the other a fashionable open-air tea salon at the beginning of the 20th century.

LES BAINS DE BRUXELLES

Pool with two views

Rue du Chevreuil 28
02 511 24 68
Monday to Friday 7.30am–7.30pm and Saturday 7.30am–5pm
Showers and baths: Tuesday to Saturday 9am–2pm
Trams 23, 52, 55 and 56, Lemonnier stop

Although close to the place du Jeu de Balle, the Bains de Bruxelles building is discreet, giving little indication of what lies in side.

It was the Brussels commune's wish to provide an indoor swimming pool in Les Marolles neighbourhood that led to the construction of this sports and sanitary facility. The marshy ground of Brussels did the builders no favours. They had to pump out 350 million litres of water in a single year in order to start construction, thus converting a veritable underground lake into a suspended swimming pool.

As the first-floor pool is reserved to school groups, swimmers in the main pool on the third floor can thus peacefully go about their business, although not without a strange sensation of levitating: the room ends in a glass wall overlooking rue des Capucins that offers an astonishing view of the towers of La Chapelle church and the neighbourhood roofs. By way of a labyrinth of stairs and hallways, you arrive at the 182 austere changing booths on the third and fourth floors.

Following the construction of the new swimming pool, the old municipal baths in rue des Tanneurs, by then already 56 years old and regarded as too dilapidated, were replaced by showers and bathtubs in the new establishment at rue du Chevreuil. Over a century ago, most households in fact lacked private sanitation and public baths were indispensable, particularly in working-class neighbourhoods such as Les Marolles.

Today, the baths and showers continue to be used by the poorest residents: despite its proximity to Les Sablons, Les Marolles is still a low-income area.

NEARBY
Institut Diderot
Rue des Capucins 58
Unfairly ignored by Brussels' residents, Institut Diderot is a beautiful school built by Henri Jacobs in 1908. Ring the doorbell at the main entrance and tell them you would like to take a look at the architecture. Hidden behind the rather plain façade, the inner courtyard is a beautiful rendition of the Art Nouveau style. Note the superb sgraffito by Privat Livemont in the courtyard. Completed in 1910, it depicts *St Michael slaying the dragon.*

The Cortvriendt House (38)
Rue de Nancy 6–8
Built in 1900 by Léon Sneyers, a pupil of Hankar, the Cortvriendt house is a pleasant surprise in this rather dull part of Les Marolles neighbourhood, with its wrought-iron balustrades and pretty sgraffiti.

FORMER ROTUNDA
OF THE PANORAMA CAR PARK

A fantastic vestige of a 19th-century panorama

Boulevard Maurice Lemonnier 10
24/7
Metro Lemonnier

E ven The Panorama car park curiously lies behind the carriage entrance of an imposing and eclectic façade. From the moment you enter the lower level, the riveted metal girders, some of which are arched, will tip you off: this is not your everyday car park but a former rotunda for a panoramic painting.

Indeed, from the moment it was built in 1879 to a design by architect Henri Rieck, the building was the setting for a vast circular painting which, like the one found today at the base of the Lion of Waterloo, depicted the Battle of Waterloo. It was the work of artist Charles Castellani.

In 1920 – given the First World War victory – this painting was replaced with another one depicting the Battle of Yser.

By 1924, however, such large panoramic paintings were no longer in fashion. The building was converted into a car park and partitioned off following contemporary practices. A fascinating trace still remains, however.

As you drive up to park on the third level, a vast 16-panel space, with a circumference of roughly 120 m, opens up before you. It is topped by an iron cupola covered in small wooden panels. This is where the pictorial spectacle was mounted and enhanced by subdued lighting. Viewers could contemplate it from the centre of the building, designed as a belvedere.

What is a panoramic painting?

The craze for 'panoramas' began at the end of the 18th century and lasted until the first quarter of the 20th century.

Both pictorial and architectural, this type of scenography aimed at recreating reality by playing with the viewer's perceptions. It consisted of a large 360° cylindrical painting mounted on the walls of a circular building and which the public could admire from a central platform.

The most frequently depicted themes were natural or urban landscapes, but also battle scenes (with a predilection for the Napoleonic wars) or biblical scenes. Brussels had another panoramic painting, dating from 1897, which depicted a view of Cairo and stood in what is now the Grand Mosque of the Parc du Cinquantenaire.

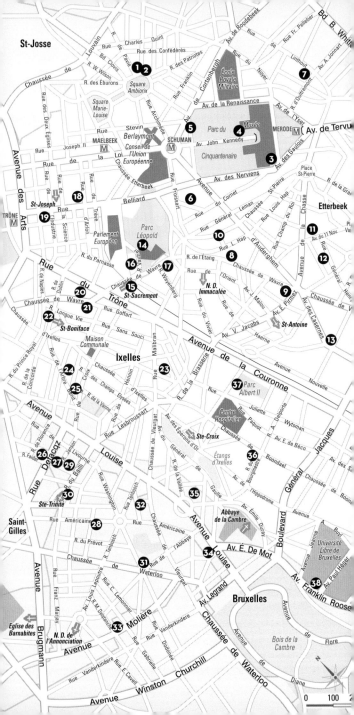

Ixelles, Etterbeek, European District

SAINT-CYR HOUSE

Extravagant

Square Ambiorix 11
Private house; closed to public
Tram No. 54 and 63, Ambiorix stop

© Trougnouf (Benoit Brummer)

Maison Saint-Cyr has one of the most beautiful Art Nouveau façades in Brussels. Built in 1903 by Gustave Strauven for the painter Georges Saint-Cyr, it is remarkable for its flamboyant and exuberant decorations, but also its narrowness: only 3.55 m wide, for a height of 19.5 m.

To cope with this narrow width, Strauven conceived a central staircase with a light well and a glass ceiling to allow natural lighting. This staircase serves various rooms, each of them decorated in a different style: you go from an Art Nouveau entry hall to a Chinese salon, then by taking the Empire-style stairs you reach the Renaissance dining room.

Gustave Strauven

Born in Schaerbeek in 1878, from 1896 to 1898 Strauven was a pupil of Victor Horta, with whom he notably worked in drafting plans for the Maison du Peuple (since demolished) and for the Hôtel Van Eetvelde, in nearby avenue Palmerston. In 1898, he left for Switzerland where he was employed by the architectural firms of Chiodra and Tshudy in Zurich. He died in 1919 at the age of 40. From 1899 to 1914, he designed some 30 buildings, most of them in the communes of Brussels (square Ambiorix), Saint-Josse and Schaerbeek.

ART NOUVEAU AROUND SQUARE AMBIORIX

Not to be missed on heritage days

Hôtel Delhaye : avenue Palmerston 2
Hôtel Deprez-Van de Velde : avenue Palmerston 3
Hôtel Van Eetvelde-maison du gaz naturel : avenue Palmerston 4
Boulevard Clovis 85
Trams No. 54 and 63, Ambiorix stop

The neighbourhood around square Ambiorix is one of the areas in Brussels with the greatest number of Art Nouveau buildings. Just beyond Maison Saint-Cyr, avenue Palmerston has three beautiful Art Nouveau townhouses designed by the master Victor Horta (1861–1947). They can only be infrequently visited, during the *journées du patrimoine* (heritage open days) held in September, or during tours organized by associations such as Arau or Arkadia.

The most famous of these townhouses is the Hôtel Van Eetvelde, built by Victor Horta between 1895 and 1897 for the former Colonial minister, Edmond Van Eetvelde. Today this building is occupied by offices of the Belgian federation of natural gas suppliers, giving rise to its present nickname, the 'maison du gaz naturel'. The house is unique for the extent of the iron work used both outside and inside, as well as the refinement of its interior decoration. If you have the chance to look around inside, note the luxurious materials employed and the stairwell cupola. At No. 2 in the same avenue, the Hôtel Delhaye was constructed between 1899 and 1900 as an extension to the Hôtel Van Eetvelde. If you manage to get in, be sure to admire the superb meeting room and the gas stove enthroned in the middle. The Hôtel Deprez-Van de Velde, opposite Hôtel Van Eetvelde, was built between 1895 and 1897. Not quite as accomplished a work as its neighbours and transformed several times since its original construction, it is of less interest to the non-architect. Just nearby, at 85 boulevard Clovis (see photo) is another building designed by Strauven in 1901 and renovated in 1989. Note the oblique positioning of the façade from the first floor upwards. Was this because Strauven wanted to provide a better view of the lively activity on the chaussée de Louvain? There are also some superb wrought-iron balconies.

A little further on, at No. 35 Rue Le Corrège, the house designed by architect Edouard Ramaekers dates from 1899. It is designed as a work of art in its own right, with exceptional stained-glass windows, sgraffito work and elaborate ironwork. At No. 31 Rue de l'Abdication, Victor Horta designed a little-known house for his friend, the sculptor Pierre Braecke. The elegant bronze handles on the carriage entrance, designed and built by the sculptor, are particularly noteworthy. Gustave Strauven's house at No. 28 Rue Luther is a real gem that was built in 1902 on a very narrow plot of land. As the house was built on a through plot, the rear façade is on Rue Calvin and is much simpler than the main façade, though it remains very tastefully designed. It can be visited during the Banad Festival days, held every year in March (dates to be checked on the Banad website).

For more information about Art Nouveau, see the following double page.

Art Nouveau

The world's Art Nouveau capital in the architectural field, Brussels boasts the very first Art Nouveau building, the Hôtel Tassel, designed by Victor Horta in 1893. It is also in Brussels where the last major work of this movement can be admired, the famous Palais Stoclet (not covered here), built between 1905 and 1911 by Joseph Hoffmann and already a precursor of Art Deco. These two buildings, along with all the other examples gathered together in Brussels, are emblematic of the two great tendencies within Art Nouveau that took hold across Europe at the beginning of the 20th century: the organic or asymmetric line whose leading figure in Belgium was Victor Horta, and the geometric line of the German Jugendstil represented by Joseph Hoffmann and the 'Wiener Werkstätte', as well as by Paul Hankar and Paul Cauchie. The term Art Nouveau owes its origin to Samuel Bing (1838–1905), an art dealer from Hamburg who in 1895 opened a gallery in Paris named 'L'Art Nouveau', where he began to exhibit work by most of the future major representatives of this new form of art.

Today applied above all to the geometric current, Jugendstil was also initially used to designate Art Nouveau in Germany and Austria. The name stems from the satirical weekly, *Jugend* (Youth), launched in 1896 by a German publisher, Georg Hirth, in Munich. Its provocative style and original typography were soon associated with numerous other artistic innovations in this period.

Other terms also closely related to Art Nouveau in Europe include: Sezessionstil in Austria, referring to the Vienna Secession movement founded by Gustav Klimt in 1897; Liberty Style in England, derived from the shop, Liberty of London, specialist dealers at this time in fabrics with modern designs; and Modern Style, which encompassed both great European tendencies. But other more popular nicknames, such as 'noodle' or 'spaghetti' style, also alluded to the same concept. More than a mere artistic movement, Art Nouveau aspired to becoming a new manner of thinking and living, which would break away from a model of society that it rejected. Its goal was liberation from a system based on the exploitation of workers, the role of the Church, and the oppression of women, by means of an eroticism and sensuality hitherto forbidden. This can be seen in the numerous stylized and sensuous representations of female heads found on the façades of houses built in this style. After having known a golden age in Brussels between 1892 and 1914, Art Nouveau came to a sudden halt with the First World War. Impossible to build on a large scale and at low cost, this style of architecture was incapable of responding to the need for mass reconstruction.

CASTING WORKSHOPS ③

For those who've always dreamed of seeing the Venus de Milo or a Roman emperor in their living room

Entrance from avenue des Nerviens, near entrance to Musées d'art et d'histoire
02 741 73 02
Individual visits on Thursdays from 1.30pm to 4 pm – Admission free

The *Ateliers de Moulage* (casting workshops) are amazing, a place beyond time and fashion that makes for a pleasant, fascinating visit. The employees are friendly and delighted to be able to share their passion for their work. With their permission, spend a moment watching them make castings. Ask them to explain the techniques they

© Jean-Jacques Evrard

use and have a look at the room where they store some 4,000 moulds. It is into such moulds that they pour the plaster in order to make statues. Lastly, ask them if you can see their storeroom full of statues, busts and other types of cast.

In addition to the tour, the workshops also have an exhibition space, plus a catalogue with a list of works of art of which you might like a copy. For those who've always dreamed of seeing the Venus de Milo or a Roman emperor in their living room, this is your chance. A male torso from the 4th century BC or a Neapolitan princess from the Italian Renaissance cost about €250, while a reproduction of Donatello's Christ on the Cross from the 15th century is priced at €300. If you're feeling even more ambitious, there's a very finely made bust of Colbert for €900, about the same as a simple statue on a plinth. All these prices include a very white, brute finish. For other patinas, you'll need to add around 50%.

But why deprive yourself, when you can acquire a Donatello statue in imitation bronze for just €500.

Founded in 1876, at about the same time as similar establishments in several other European cities, notably London, Paris and Athens, the Ateliers de Moulage were created with the educational aim of allowing people to discover the masterpieces of world sculpture without having to travel halfway round the world to see them. Once they came into being, the British Museum, the Louvre, and the museums of Athens and Brussels began to exchange moulds and castings from their own collections. In Brussels as in these other cities, numerous famous pieces became accessible to apprentice sculptors who could practise their art with these plasters before undertaking real works of their own.

© Jean-Jacques Evrard

Another more unexpected use of the workshops was to reconstitute originals that had been lost, stolen or destroyed. One such case was the famous shrine of St Gertrude that melted in the flames of the bombardment of Nivelles during the Second World War. Moulds from the Ateliers meant that the original could be reconstituted.

PANORAMIC TERRACES OF THE CINQUANTENAIRE ARCADE

Generous donators who served as frontmen
for Leopold II ...

Parc du Cinquantenaire 3
02 737 78 33 – klm-mra.be
Free admission through the Royal Museum of the Armed Forces and Military
History
Daily 9am–12pm and 1pm–4.45pm; closed Monday and some public holidays
Metro Mérode

Whether you want to impress your partner or show off in front of visiting friends, the panoramic terraces of the Cinquantenaire arcade are most certainly a good bet. Located on either side of the quadriga entitled *Brabant Raising the National Flag*, they offer a 360° panorama of Brussels and illustrate the arcade's role as a 'gateway' to this part of the city. You can see the Royal Park on one side and the foliage of the Soignes Forest on the other.

The arcade, which is 60 m wide and 40 m high, is built in blue stone on a concrete foundation. It presents a veritable catalogue of late 19th-century Belgian sculpture. Its tumultuous history covers twenty-five years. Indeed, the exorbitant construction costs kept the authorities from carrying through the project, despite the insistence of Leopold II.

Designed by architect Gédéon Bordiau for the Exhibition celebrating the 50th anniversary of Belgian independence in 1880, the arcade originally had only one arch, built simply from wood and plaster. In 1890, they contemplated rebuilding it in stronger materials, in view of the World Exhibition of 1897, but the funds allocated for the project turned out to be insufficient. Only the concrete uprights were completed and, once again, they supported arches made of temporary materials. In 1904, Leopold II decided to finish the arcade using his own money in preparation for the ceremonies of Belgium's 75th anniversary. Using frontmen known as the 'generous donators', he financed all the construction, paying out of his own pocket and with revenue from the Congo (hence the arcade's nickname of the 'missing hands', invented by those who opposed the brutal policies of the king's governors in Africa).

Unfortunately Bordiau the architect died in 1904, so Leopold turned to Frenchman Charles Girault, the designer of the Petit Palais in Paris. Girault modified Bordiau's project and proposed a triple arcade that was better suited to a city gateway and to the dimensions of avenue de Tervueren. They thus began by dynamiting the existing uprights. Just eight months after the beginning of construction work, the arcade was inaugurated in September 1905. If you take the stairs, on one of the landings you'll find an exhibit of old photographs showing the various stages of the Cinquantenaire arcade and palaces.

THE TEMPLE
OF HUMAN PASSIONS

⑤

*Representing a tangle of naked bodies, the sculpture
was condemned as an outrage to decency*

By the Schumann round about, next to the mosque
*Tuesday to Friday 2.30pm–3.30pm (Tuesday to Sunday 2.30pm–4.30pm May
to September inclusive)*
Tickets sold at the cash desk in the nearby Musée du Cinquantenaire
Metro Schumann

Commissioned by the Belgian state in 1890, the high relief created by sculptor Jef Lambeaux (1852–1908) is one of the public works of art least familiar to the residents of the capital. And for good cause: when it was unveiled in 1898 it caused an immediate scandal. Representing a tangle of naked bodies, it was condemned as immoral and an outrage to decency. The *Pavillon des Passions Humaines* that housed it was forced to close its doors three days later. And it has never really reopened. Since 2004, however, the situation has evolved slightly: you need to make an explicit request to the cashier at the *Musées Royaux d'Art et d'Histoire* in order to have any hope of seeing the inside of the pavilion.

The notorious sculpture is still to be seen within the small temple designed by Victor Horta. This neoclassical building was the first public edifice built by the young architect and fails to match any of the Art Nouveau masterpieces of his more mature period. Nevertheless, it does contain this crowning artistic achievement by Jef Lambeaux, an ode to life and gaiety rarely equalled in its power and intensity.

NEARBY

Impasse du Pré 32 ⑥

Next to rue Jean-André de Mot 31

A rustic impasse that curves to the right, lined with small, two-storey houses for workers built around 1850 and restored.

RECEPTION OF THE SAINT-MICHEL HOSPITAL

A futuristic entrance

Rue de Linthout 130

On entering the Saint-Michel Hospital, someone might think that s/he has arrived at the wrong address. Not in the least: rather than settling for a classic hospital entrance, the Saint-Michel authorities have in fact chosen to create an entrance hall worthy of a science fiction film. In order to do this, they have called upon the services of Antoine Pinto – an interior designer famous for his work in cafes and restaurants – for the designing of the reception. In addition to the flying saucer that serves as an office for the reception staff, Pinto has designed the hospital brasserie in the same futuristic style. Of particular interest is the recess housing a table isolated from the rest of the restaurant. Also of interest are the coloured fluorescent lines embedded in the ground, which help people to find the correct room or department.

NEARBY
Hap Park

Chaussée de Wavre 510
Bus No. 34, Fétis

A small urban park slightly larger than a hectare in size, situated between chaussée de Wavre and chaussée d'Auderghem, the Hap Park is one of Etterbeek's best kept secrets, a short distance from the European Union institutions.

Inside the park, a real oasis in the centre of the city, there are hundred-year-old trees, a pond, a pavilion, an old orangery, a large lawn, the spring of the Broebelaer stream as well as public benches to which small plaques have been fixed in memory of users who have passed away.

In 1804, Albert-Joseph Hap, an industrialist who was mayor of the Etterbeek district, decided to acquire a large plot of ground alongside the Broebelaer stream. His son, François-Louis Hap, who was not only a lawyer but also mayor of the district, built a residence that can still be seen from the park, although unfortunately it is in very bad condition. His grandson, Jean-Félix Hap, inherited the estate and created a park there, which was left to the commune in 1988 on the death of his own son, Jean Hap.

ALBERT HALL COMPLEX

Two superb Art Deco halls: cinema and ballroom

Chaussée de Wavre 649/651
02 649 98 89
albert-hall.com
Trams No. 81 and 82, Chasse stop

It's easy to pass by the Albert Hall complex without suspecting even for a second the existence of the architectural treasure that lies behind this façade well-aligned with all the others along the street.

Nevertheless, inside there are two superb Art Deco halls with a total surface area of 2,500 m². Although in principle not open to the public, these rooms can be hired and are thus accessible to those interested in seeing them.

It was in 1932 that the architect Meuleman designed both 'Le Roseland' ballroom and 'L'Albert Hall'. As the functions of these halls didn't need natural light, the 'underground' atmosphere within the complex gives an unusual touch to the handsome decor of wrought iron, gilded stucco and sgraffiti with floral motifs. Closed in 1965, the complex was renovated 30 years later.

Le Roseland is perfect for dance lovers: two balconies, one just above the floor and the other at mezzanine level, overlook the parquet dance floor of 150 m². You'll also notice, in the entrance hall, two stained-glass windows representing Charlie Chaplin and Virginia Cherrill in the film *City Lights*.

NEARBY

Impasse de la Chaussée Saint-Pierre 56

An attractive little passage lined with rustic housing.

Avenue de la Chasse 141

Less well known than the Maison Cauchic at 5 rue des Francs, this house is also the work of architect Paul Cauchie. Dating back to 1910, it has a pretty sgraffito with two female figures seated in the centre of a floral design. It has survived thanks to owners Guy and Léo Dessicy who saved it from destruction and carried out restoration work.

Cité Jouet-Rey

Entrances opposite rue des Cultivateurs 35 and rue du Général Henry 14

The Cité Jouet-Rey (built in 1909–10 at the behest of the Hospices de Bruxelles) is divided into 32 brick dwellings, forming a little village right in the heart of the Belgian capital. The ensemble has a rather rustic appearance, organized around a very pleasant central green. On fine days, residents bring out lounge chairs or spread themselves out on the thick grass, beneath the gaze of rare visitors who may want to linger on one of the convenient benches and soak up the tranquil atmosphere.

The Cité is occupied by three associations in aid of the elderly, the sick and people in difficulty.

Descend into the history of crime

Avenue de la Force aérienne 33
CGC@police.belgium.eu
Monday to Friday, 9am–12pm and 1.30pm–4.30pm
We suggest a guided tour, available for groups of 15 or more by reservation: call
02 642 69 29
You can include a visit to the Gendarmerie's stables or a democratic lunch in
the mess hall
Trams No. 23, 24 and 25, Deuxième Lanciers stop

Behind one of the stern façades of the Casernes (Barracks) neighbourhood in Etterbeek lies the surprising Police Museum. The visit begins rather traditionally by evoking the origin of the police. In the modern sense of the term, this police force is a relatively recent invention that was set up under French rule in 1794 and that included three forces: the gendarmerie (national law enforcement service), the municipal police, and the judicial police. This history punctuated by technical advances (the evolution of wheeled vehicles, for example), changes in mentality (such as the incorporation of women in the late 1960s), and organizational modifications (police reforms, etc.) is presented on the ground floor and illustrated by a large number of mannequins. Although this section is informative and interesting, the heart of the museum is on the upper floor.

The museum of the former national school of criminology and crime detection, better known as the Crime Museum, which was formerly located in the maze of the Brussels law courts, was transferred here a few years ago. Various pieces of evidence from both trivial and important cases are reunited in a relative chaos that accentuates the abundant and unsettling aspects of the history of crime in this country. Here, you'll find amusing objects like the little gadgets believed to exist only in the imagination of novelists: sword canes, umbrellas with blades, a book serving as a hiding place for a revolver, a stiletto pen, a mobile phone concealing a tazer, and more. Nor has counterfeiting been left out, with a multitude of exhibits illustrating the ingenuity of counterfeiters and a collection of copied masterpieces, from Khnopff to Somville, recuperated by the art brigade. The tools of a perfect safe-cracker or the techniques of a pickpocket are also terribly interesting.

The museum, in a true reflection of reality, also has a few shadier exhibits, from the soundproofed box in which a young Swedish woman was imprisoned for four full days in 1993 to a foetus kept in a jar of formaldehyde, a piece of evidence from a time when abortion was still illegal. The most macabre exhibit, however, is the collection of fifteen death masks of prisoners executed by guillotine. They were made in the hopes of establishing a physiognomic theory of assassins – a typical scientific craze in the 19th century.

THE SOLVAY LIBRARY

Industrialist Ernest Solvay made the library
his 'brain factory'

Parc Léopold
Rue Belliard 137
Visits during occasional exhibitions or by arrangement – 02 738 75 96
Bus No. 12, 21, 27 and 59, Parc Léopold stop

You'll need to follow the winding paths of Parc Léopold to find the small jewel of the Solvay Library. Built in 1901 by Constant Bosmans and Henri Vandeveld, this library completed a vast project creating a scientific complex in the park (five institutes and research laboratories), isolated from the noise of the surrounding city. The industrialist Ernest Solvay was the driving force behind the whole scheme: the library became his 'brain factory' and a laboratory for his scientific and political ideas. But this great dream came to an end in 1919 when the university abandoned the monumental buildings and moved to the Solbosch campus.

After having been squatted for many years, the library was renovated in 2004 and now houses various European associations as well as hosting a number of events. In the central hall, which has a beautiful curved vault, you can readily imagine the quiet, studious atmosphere of the library's former years, particularly when you see the individual study carrels behind the doors lining the gallery. Double natural lighting (from above and the sides) highlights the precious woods, mosaics, stained glass and painted decor.

NEARBY

'Bruxelles Europe à ciel ouvert' Campground

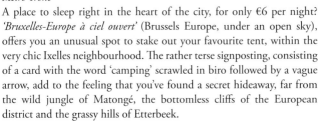

Chaussée de Wavre 203
02 640 79 67
Only during July and August
Métro Trône

A place to sleep right in the heart of the city, for only €6 per night? *'Bruxelles-Europe à ciel ouvert'* (Brussels Europe, under an open sky), offers you an unusual spot to stake out your favourite tent, within the very chic Ixelles neighbourhood. The rather terse signposting, consisting of a card with the word 'camping' scrawled in biro followed by a vague arrow, add to the feeling that you've found a secret hideaway, far from the wild jungle of Matongé, the bottomless cliffs of the European district and the grassy hills of Etterbeek.

To reach it, go to Saint-Sacrement church then make your way to a car park up a slope, where you'll see the entrance to the campsite. A patch of open ground consisting of a pretty lawn dotted with trees and flowers, yet surrounded by tall buildings, this land used to belong to the youth hostel on chaussée de Wavre. The garden was bought by the Viale Europe community seven years ago. It is practically next door to Place Royale and the Saint-Boniface district and very near to the city centre itself. The campsite can accommodate 50 tents. If this refuge in the greenery inspires you, the nearby church holds Masses or other services every day, at noon and in the evening.

WIERTZ MUSEUM

Unrecognized by his peers, the painter Antoine Wiertz wanted to be 'Rubens or nothing'

Rue Vautier 62
02 648 17 18
Tuesday to Friday 10am–12pm and 1pm–5pm
Admission free
Bus No. 34, 38, 54, 59 and 95

Hidden away in a back street behind the Museum of Natural Science, the Wiertz Museum is one of the most unusual museums in Brussels. Located in the former studio of the Belgian painter Antoine Wiertz (1806–65), it is given over entirely to the monumental paintings by this artist. Despite the impressive size of the main studio, it has a warm, intimate atmosphere that gives visits a special quality.

Antoine Wiertz, who was detested by most of his peers because of his inherently large ego, had a revelation when he gazed on Rubens' famous *Descent from the Cross* in Antwerp for the first time. From that moment, he wanted to follow in the footsteps of the great Baroque painter ('be Rubens or nothing'), and according to critics some of the force of the grand master from Antwerp does seem to have found its way into Wiertz's own work. Wiertz, suffering from various personal setbacks, wanted above all to leave his mark – he was convinced that 'to judge a painter, you need to wait two centuries at least'. So, he decided to turn his future and final studio into a museum. In March 1850, he revealed his plan to Charles Rogier, the Belgian Minister of the Interior at the time. In exchange for a promise that he would bequeath his work to the Belgian state, he managed to persuade the government to fund the construction of a vast studio. Its dimensions (35 m long, 15 m wide and 16 m high) at last gave Wiertz enough space to complete his monumental canvasses. It's true that the size of some of his paintings is bemusing. His *La Chute des anges rebelles* (Fall of the Rebel Angels), for example, measures 11.53 m by 7.93 m. Wiertz died in the museum he had created around him in 1865. As agreed, in his will he left all his work to the Belgian state and the museum opened its doors to the public the same year.

Containing nearly 220 paintings by Wiertz, it now forms part of the Royal Museums of Fine Arts of Belgium, which explains why admission is free, as in the case of the Constantin Meunier Museum. That's just one more reason to visit this place off the beaten tourist track that is especially convenient to EU staff who may not even realize that this museum is only a short walk from their offices, just across the beautiful Leopold Park.

NEARBY

Rue Wayenberg 12-22

A pretty cobbled inner courtyard.

LE CONCERT NOBLE

A former society for meeting members of the nobility

Rue d'Arlon 82
02 286 41 51
info@concertnoble.com
Daily 9am–4pm

inding a place like this in the middle of the European district, among modern buildings of varying quality, is quite a surprise. A former society for meeting members of the nobility, the Concert Noble is today an ensemble of prestigious reception rooms that can be hired to host events for up to 650 people. Which also means that it can be visited by the public. It was in 1873, under the sponsorship of King Leopold II, that the Société du Concert Noble built these meeting rooms in the Léopold neighbourhood, where the Belgian nobility tended to have their urban residences.

The architect Hendrik Beyaert came up with a unique concept: he created a set of rooms that gradually increased in size, from the gallery to the impressive ballroom, all in a majestic fashion. The eye is drawn to a series of tapestries and a grand portrait of King Leopold II and Queen Marie-Louise, along with furniture mainly in the Directoire style (1795–99).

© Zinneke

CONCERTS IN PAINTER MARCEL HASTIR'S STUDIO

Hastirix versus the invaders

Rue du Commerce 51
Drawing class on Monday afternoon – 0486 107 167
Frequent concerts – 02 281 78 85 (during the day)
ateliermarcelhastir.eu – ateliermarcelhastir@gmail.com
Metro Trône

Miraculously spared thanks to one man's tenacity, the studio of artist Marcel Hastir, who is 104 years old, is a veritable time machine.

Here, we go back to a time before the Leopold district became the office-filled, traffic-ridden business district that it is today, when the upper crust of the nobility and bourgeoisie of the Belgium of yesteryear filled it with their mansions, each one more luxurious than the next.

In 1935, this house, built in 1860 for an officer of the court of Leopold II (the fencing, dancing and gym room was added around 1900), became the home of a young painter of portraits, nudes and landscapes who had completed classical training at the Académie des Beaux-Arts in Brussels. A strong believer in humanism and spirituality, Marcel Hastir was a theosophist.

When the Second World War broke out, Marcel soon chose his side. His art studio, posing as a school of painting, was used to keep young adults from being sent to work camps in Germany and to keep Jews out of the clutches of the Holocaust. He used his own artistic talents to create and supply fake papers.

A humanist painter and figure of the Resistance, Marcel Hastir is also an extraordinary cultural activist. For over 70 years, he has organized concerts at his home (over 2,000, he reckons). Performers such as Barbara and Jacques Brel made their débuts here, and the famous Queen Elisabeth Competition was born in collaboration with the queen, who was one of his art students. At his advanced age, Marcel Hastir will outlive himself thanks to a public interest foundation and a non-profit organization that have succeeded in keeping his home out of the greedy hands of promoters. Thanks to these organizations, drawing classes (every Monday afternoon) and concerts are still held today in the painter's studio, gathering more than 70 people among the old master's monumental portraits and nudes. These are extraordinary moments when time fades and art fully rediscovers its calling – that of transcending time and of bringing together artists and spectators around a place and a work.

CAMILLE LEMONNIER MUSEUM

A writer who stood up for his own work ...

Chaussée du Wavre 150
02 512 29 68
Every day of the week 10am–12pm and 2pm–4pm or by arrangement
Metro Porte de Namur

A visit to this museum devoted to the work of Camille Lemonnier (1844–1913) is a moment to be savoured, thanks mainly to the graciousness of the curator, Émile Kesteman, who insists on personally providing a guided tour.

Probably because he understands that it isn't easy to visit a writer's museum without someone to provide commentary. His passion and enthusiasm make even the smallest details concerning the lives of Camille Lemonnier and his entourage captivating.

Installed on the first floor of the Maison des Écrivains Belges, the museum was set up in 1946 thanks to the collection bequeathed by Marie Lemonnier, the master's elder daughter.

It still retains an extremely pleasant, intimate atmosphere.

Armed with an encyclopaedic knowledge of his subject, Monsieur Kesteman will lead you through the three rooms, filled with souvenirs linked to the writer: paintings by some of his friends and associates (Constantin Meunier, Van Rysselberghe…), as well as by his own hand; a library composed of 53 magnificent volumes illustrated by numerous Belgian artists such as Claus, Ensor and Knopf; a statue by Rodin; and also a portrait of the author which reveals that like Hemingway, Victor Hugo and Erasmus, Lemonnier wrote standing up.

ÉTABLISSEMENTS DEMEULDRE

One of the finest windows in Brussels

Chaussée de Wavre 141–143
02 511 51 44
Tuesday to Saturday 9.30am–6.30pm

É tablissements Demeuldre has one of the finest shop windows in the entire Brussels region. Created in 1904 by architect Maurice Bisschops, a pupil of Horta, Belgium's grand master of Art Nouveau, it inevitably draws your eye and invites you to step inside the shop. You'll discover a magnificent wooden counter, and above all, lining the staircase, some beautiful ceramic panels created in 1880 by Isidore de Rudder, with allegories of music, colour and architecture. Founded in 1830 by the Lorraine porcelain manufacturer, Charles-Christophe

© Jean-Jacques Evrard

Windisch, Établissements Demeuldre was a major supplier of ceramics for over a century. Taken over by M.A. Caillet in 1842, and passing to the Vermeren-Coché couple in 1852, the company was finally bought in 1900 by the Demeuldre-Coché family. Expanded several times, these premises have housed the firm's retail shop since the end of the 19th century. Production ceased in 1953, and the workshop where the ceramics were made was demolished in 1960. Among the firm's greatest achievements are the external decorations for the former Old England department store at Le Mont des Arts and the decor created by Victor Horta for the *Maison du Peuple*, which was also razed in the 1960s. Since the halt in production by the company, the shop in chaussée de Wavre limits itself to selling porcelain, crystal, gold and silver work, also tableware. The shop's present director, Françoise Demeuldre-Coché, is a descendant of the original founder.

ART NOUVEAU FAÇADES
IN SAINT-BONIFACE

A feast of Art Nouveau

Rue Solvay and Rue Saint-Boniface
Metro Porte de Namur

I t's rather surprising to find so many extraordinary Art Nouveau façades in the Saint-Boniface neighbourhood.

On 15 July 1898, the commune of Ixelles launched a competition for façades with a prize of 15,000 Belgian francs, hoping to improve the quality of housing in a neighbourhood that was just starting to be built. This encouraged Ernest Blérot and several of his colleagues to carry out various Art Nouveau projects in rue Saint-Boniface and rue Solvay.

Blérot built these houses in 1900, the same year as his remarkable ensemble in rue Vanderscrik at Saint-Gilles. The architect managed to complete both these projects, with a total of 28 dwellings, in a relatively short time thanks to his standardized methods: the interior layout was always the same and associated with one of five possible types of façade, although their appearance varied due to the diversity of sgraffiti.

Eleven examples of Blérot's work are to be found in this neighbourhood: No. 12 in rue Solvay, which long remained the property of Blérot himself and is now owned by one of his descendants; the houses at Nos. 14, 16, 18, 20 and 22; and lastly No. 19, whose sgraffito has unfortunately been restored in overly bright colours, probably the result of using acrylics. No. 17 in rue Saint-Boniface has pretty balconies and two sgraffiti somewhat hidden beneath white paint, representing Romeo and Juliet in medieval costumes, and Nos. 19, 20, and 22 also have nice sgraffiti, although the one at No. 20 is badly deteriorated. No. 22 features some beautiful balconies, too.

Among the other Art Nouveau homes in the area, the most spectacular are probably those at Nos. 33, 35 and 37 rue Solvay, at the junction with rue Longue-Vie. Built by Antoine Dujardin in 1900, they are decorated with a total of 13 sgraffiti attributed to Géo Ponchon, located at first-floor level but obscured by dark grey paint.

Finally, we should mention the house built in 1904 by architect Victor Taelemans at 32 rue Solvay. This was his fifth and last building project, and is distinguishable from other Art Nouveau homes nearby by its geometrical tendencies, closer in spirit to the work of Paul Hankar or the artists belonging to the Vienna Secession movement.

SGRAFFITI OF
THE MAISON DRICOT

Outstanding sgraffiti depicting construction workers

Rue Malibran 47

© Jean-Jacques Evrard

Designed by Edmond Pelseneer in 1900 for building contractor Pierre Dricot, the house at No. 47 Rue Malibran is a magnificent, Art Nouveau-style, bourgeois building.

The most striking feature, of course, is the excellent sgraffito work by Paul Cauchie, depicting the trades practised by the owner's company.

They show seven construction workers in action, with their tools and materials.

Like the well-known façade Cauchie created for himself and his wife on Rue des Francs in Etterbeek, this one can be seen as a genuine advertisement, clearly serving as a business card for the contractor Dricot.

The sgraffiti were remarkably restored to their original design in 2017, thanks to subsidies from the Brussels Region. The rest of the facade had undergone destructive renovations in the 1980s, including the replacement of the original loggias. Today, it has almost entirely been restored to its former glory.

NEARBY

Rue Souveraine 52 (24)

A beautiful Art Nouveau house built by Gustave Strauven in 1902, and one of the few works by this architect to be found outside Schaerbeek and the squares of the Quartier de l'Europe. You'll notice that an extra storey has been added to the original house. Admirers of Strauven should also see the famous Saint-Cyr house at 11 square Ambiorix, as well as the house at 85 boulevard Clovis (see p. 108 and 110).

Géo Ponchon's Studio (25)

Rue de la Croix 25

An old neoclassical building that displays three panels of sgraffiti, well-drawn but in poor condition. Ponchon, who himself produced sgraffiti, devised a system to prevent them from deteriorating through time and exposure to the elements. Since his customers were often put off by the need to completely restore a sgraffito at great expense every few years, he proposed instead to carry out regular maintenance work in return for an annual subscription.

© Rebexho

THREE HOUSES
BY PAUL HANKAR
RUE DEFACQZ

The best of a major Art Nouveau architect

Rue Defacqz 48, 50 and 71
Trams No. 92 and 93

© Trougnouf (Benoit Brummer)

Rue Defacqz, just a few steps from avenue Louise, offers visitors three Art Nouveau residences by the architect Paul Hankar (1859–1901). The most remarkable of these is the Ciamberlani house at No. 48. Built in 1897 and listed in 1983, it was commissioned by the painter Albert Ciamberlani (1894–1956), a descendant from a noble family in Bologna, Italy. The painter took part in decorating the Palais de Justice in Brussels and was also responsible for some mosaics beneath the Arcades du Cinquantenaire. Six of his paintings are now in Brussels' Musée des Beaux-Arts.

Working with an unusual building width of 12 m, Hankar achieved the most successful construction of his entire career. Despite a certain austerity, the façade is pleasing in its originality and sgraffiti. The two big windows in the shape of horseshoes are very innovative for their time.

Designed by Ciamberlani, the sgraffiti were engraved by Adolphe Crespin, Hankar's traditional partner. Those at the top of the façade consist of seven medallions representing the labours of Hercules. They stand out from a decorative background of sunflowers bursting from six vases.

The sgraffiti on the first floor represent an idyllic scene in which nude bodies are entwined with nature: trees, foliage and stylized fruit. Peacocks, the symbol of the beauty, are perched on a tree.

Just next door, the house at No. 50 was also designed by Hankar. This was the home of the painter Réné Janssens (1870–1936) whose work is exhibited at the Musée des Beaux-Arts. It is not quite as accomplished as its neighbour. A little further along the street, at No. 71, you'll find the private home of Paul Hankar. Built in 1893 and listed in 1975, it was his first major work, as he made his break with classical architecture.

Its originality, notably its use of wrought iron in the façade, caused Hector Guimard, the leading light of the Art Nouveau movement in France, to pay a visit. Note the coloured sgraffiti, each representing different times of day: dawn (the rooster), daytime (the pigeon), dusk (the swallow), and night (the bat, seen against a starry sky).

The interiors of these three buildings, however, are rather less interesting.

© Jean-Jacques Evrard

Paul Hankar (1859–1901)

Influenced by his father, a stone carver, the Art Nouveau architect Paul Hankar chiefly made his reputation for the decorative aspect of his work, without attempting to re-invent traditional interior architecture. Limited to the treatment of the façades, Hankar's buildings were more readily accepted by the wider public, who liked the sgraffiti and the sculptures created by his two favourite working partners: Alphonse Crespin and Alfred Crick. In contrast to Horta and his more organic designs, Paul Hankar championed a more geometric style of Art Nouveau, well before the work of the Scot Charles Rennie Mackintosh became known in the rest of Europe. Lastly, Hankar was one of a number of architects who introduced so-called Japonisme into his building work. This consisted simply of the use of artistic forms and representations from Japan, following the opening of that country to the West in the 1860s. Adopting the stylized treatment of trees, plants and flowers, while reducing the human figure to a decorative motif, it corresponded perfectly with the spirit of Art Nouveau that had begun to develop. Despite his premature death at the age of 42, Paul Hankar was one of the major architects in the Art Nouveau movement.

Buildings by Hankar mentioned in this guidebook include: 48, 50 and 71, rue Defacqz; and the façade of 13, rue Royale.

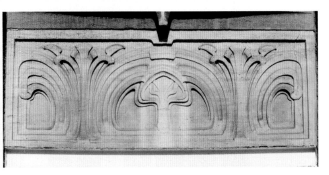

TWO BEAUTIFUL HOUSES, RUE FAIDER

*The sgraffiti around the bedroom windows are
an allegory of sleep*

Rue Faider 10 and 83
Trams No. 92 and 93

At 83 rue Faider is a superb private residence built in 1900 by
architect Albert Roosenboom (1871–1941). A draughtsman at the
studio of Victor Horta in 1896, Roosenboom was greatly inspired by
his master in the construction of this Art Nouveau work, listed in 1981.
Note in particular the original bow window on the first floor and the
attractive sgraffiti at the top of the house, attributed to Privat Livemont.
Surrounding the windows of one of the bedrooms, they probably

© Jean-Jacques Evrard

represent an allegory of sleep. At the centre of the composition, a woman puts a finger to her lips as if shushing us, while stars symbolize the night, and throughout the sgraffito, poppy flowers with their undoubted sleep-inducing properties enliven the plants entwined in the woman's hair.

Down the street at No. 10 there is another beautiful house in a more classical style by Octave van Rysselberghe, the architect of the Observatoire Royal at Uccle. Built in 1882–83 for Count Goblet d'Alviella, it was finally occupied by the architect himself until 1888. Amidst some astonishing Greco-Roman ornamentation there lies a pretty medallion representing the goddess Minerva, the work of Julien Dillens. Above it, a sgraffiti frieze shows Neptune calming a stormy sea, based on drawings by the same artist. It was engraved by Jean Baes in a very sober black-and-white that respects the traditions of the Italian Renaissance. Lastly, on the second floor, in the middle of the colonnade, is a sgraffito showing a young woman with a plumbline in her hand, a symbol of the principle of rectitude in architecture.

© Jean-Jacques Evrard

THE D'IETEREN FAMILY'S PRIVATE MUSEUM

The history of the automobile illustrated by a family's compelling rise

D'Ieteren Gallery
Rue du Mail 50
02 536 56 80
Group visits from Monday to Saturday
Bus No. 60, Washington stop, or tram No. 94, Bailli stop

Well-known to car enthusiasts, the logo of the D'Ieteren company proudly displays a carriage stamped with the date 1805. This simple logo evokes an incredible industrial and commercial adventure in the automobile industry that began in the early 19th century with the fabrication of wheels and horse-drawn vehicles, which has been led by the same family for six generations. Inside the company's astonishing and still very modern headquarters at the corner of rue du Mail and rue Américaine (designed by architect René Stapels in 1962, this building hasn't aged at all), a fabulous private museum where you can book a visit presents the extraordinary rise of this family and the diversification of the firm's activities over the years, with its highs (making the right decisions in pivotal periods) and lows (injudicious decisions, good ideas that turned out to be bad), all illustrated by a fantastic collection of vintage cars and rare iconographical documents.

2001 Lamborghini

Indeed, by itself D'Ieteren epitomizes the entire evolution of the transport industry. Over time, what began as a small-scale company of craftsmen became an industrial and commercial firm. In the early 20th century, the company, which was an official supplier for the royal family, started to manufacture car bodies, exporting a large part of its production. It then began importing and assembling cars and trucks. After the Second World War, it acquired the exclusive importation rights for Studebaker (1945), Volkswagen (1948) and Porsche (1950).

In 1956, the firm expanded to a new sector by offering Volkswagen Beetles for hire on the Belgian market. D'Ieteren subsequently started to import and to distribute other makes of the Volkswagen group in Belgium: Audi (1974), Seat (1984), Skoda (1992), Bentley (2000) and Lamborghini (2001), as well as Yamaha motorcycles and scooters (1975), all while continuing to expand its car rental activities.

NEARBY
Jardin Faider 🄴
Rue Faider 86
Daily, 9am–8pm from 1 April to 31 August; 9am–6pm from September 1st to October 31st; and 9am–5pm from November 1st to March 31st
A short walk from the noisy avenue Louise, the Jardin Faider is a welcome haven of peace in this commercial neighbourhood. The entrance is so well-hidden that this park is even unknown to many local residents. It's a godsend to come to this quiet spot to let your children play or simply sit on a bench enjoying a sandwich.

A relocated façade 🄴
Although the Church of the Holy Trinity (Sainte-Trinité) was erected on this site at the end of the 19th century while the area was being developed, its baroque façade dates from the 17th century. The latter was in fact dismantled stone by stone at its original location (place de Brouckère) during the creation of the central boulevards. The transplant has never been entirely successful since the Church of the Holy Trinity has subsequently experienced significant stability problems, to the extent that metal tie rods and girders have been installed in order to prevent any accidents.

CONSTANTIN MEUNIER MUSEUM

Over 150 paintings and sculptures in an intimate and pleasant space

Rue de l'Abbaye 59
02 648 44 49
Tuesday to Friday, 10am–12pm and 1pm–5pm and on alternate Sundays
Admission free
Trams No. 92 and 93

The Musée Constantin-Meunier is a small but charming museum that presents, as its name suggests, the works of the painter and sculptor Constantin Meunier (1831–1905).

Having finally achieved international recognition, he had his home and studio built here, where he spent the last five years of his life. Acquired by the Belgian state in 1936, the residence was opened to the public in 1939, and renovated in 1986. It now displays more than 150 paintings and sculptures in an intimate and pleasant space. Centred around a pretty little garden, the house actually possessed two studios, one of modest size facing south and another bigger one for monumental sculptures, looking to the north.

Specializing in the representation of industrial life in Belgium, notably its iron and steel mills at the end of the 19th century, Constantin Meunier is today acknowledged as one of his country's great sculptors of that period. Note that admission to this museum is free. The administrators of the Museums of Fine Arts in Belgium concluded that the museum's size and attendance did not justify the cost of charging visitors.

NEARBY

Parc Buchholtz

Three different entrances: rue Buchholtz between Nos. 1 and 15 ; rue Forestière between Nos. 22 and 24 ; rue Américain between Nos. 186 and 188
Daily 9am–8pm from April 1st to August 31st; 9am–6pm from September 1st to October 31st; and 9am–4pm from November 1st to March 31st

A short distance from Parc Tenbosch, this park is smaller and less well-known than its neighbour, one reason being that its three entrances are all practically invisible from the street. Although it is surrounded by rather dreary buildings, this is a very pleasant spot to take a rest, lulled by birdsong.

Art Deco window

Avenue Molière 256

A beautiful Art Deco stained-glass window by Armand Paulis nicely decorates this building constructed by the architect F. Petit in 1927.

STATUE OF JEAN DE SELYS LONGCHAMPS

A forgotten Brussels resident who flew over avenue Louise and bombed the Gestapo headquarters

Avenue Louise 453
Trams No. 94 and 93, Legrand stop

In the middle of the stream of cars on avenue Louise, a golden bust placed on a blue stone plinth does not appear to attract any attention. It nevertheless recalls a heroic feat of arms undertaken by a Belgian pilot during the Second World War. Jean de Selys Longchamps was a pilot in the Belgian army who, after the Belgian capitulation, succeeded in reaching London, where he joined the Royal Air Force. He regularly flew over Belgium during his missions and, in 1943, decided, without his commander's permission, to change his route in order to fly over avenue Louise at very low altitude, a street that he knew very well as a resident of Brussels. The route was not chosen at random by the pilot since he then bombed the Brussels headquarters of the Gestapo, which was located in the building at number 453 on avenue Louise. This act of bravery saw him demoted for insubordination but also, in an act of supreme irony, awarded the Royal Air Force Flying Cross. He died several months later during another mission during which his aircraft was hit.

If you would like to find out more about this act of bravery, read the comic strip *Le groom vert-de-gris, Une aventure de Spirou et Fantasio* (The Grey-Green Bellboy, A Spirou and Fantasio Adventure). The authors of this comic strip (Yann and Olivier Schwartz) had the excellent idea of including this story, which only the oldest Brussels residents are familiar with, in a Spirou and Fantasio adventure set during the Nazi occupation.

In addition to the bust of Selys, a plaque fixed to the building at 453 avenue Louise quietly recalls the former presence of the Gestapo at this location.
The cellars of the building also contained prisons in which many members of the Resistance were imprisoned.
The prisoners carved messages on the walls of their cells.
These inscriptions, which are unprotected, still exist today but are not accessible to the public.

ART NOUVEAU WALK AROUND ÉTANGS D'IXELLES

A few gems ...

Avenue Louise 346 – Rue de Belle-Vue 30, 32, 42, 44, 46,
Avenue du Général de Gaulle 38–39 – Rue Vilain XIIII 9 et 11
Rue du Lac 6
Trams No. 92 and 93

© Jean-Jacques Evrard

The Étangs d'Ixelles neighbourhood has a small number of Art Nouveau buildings, only some worth visiting casually. We propose here a selected tour that includes the most interesting.

At 346 avenue Louise you'll find the Hôtel Max Hallet. Built by Horta in 1903, this is by no means the most spectacular house from the master of Art Nouveau, but the quality of construction and of the materials used are still admirable. It is sometimes open for guided tours (www.asbl-arkadia.be; Tel. 02 563 61 53) or for events (www.events-at-horta.be).

Continuing along avenue Louise towards the Bois de la Cambre, turn left on rue Belle-Vue. At No. 42, 44 and 46, you'll come across three houses built by the architect Blérot in 1899. They are remarkable above all for the unusual character of their corbelled balconies, the curbased arches above the doors and windows, and the originality of the doors themselves with their wrought-iron grilles. There are some pretty graffiti at No. 42. A short distance away are two other eye-catching works by Blérot at No. 30 and 32, also notable for their sgraffiti.

When you reach the end of this avenue, turn left onto avenue du Général-de-Gaulle. At No. 38–39 is yet another project by Blérot (1904), but in a different style. More sober in appearance, these twin houses stand out mainly for the curving lines of their wrought-iron balustrades, and the mosaic paving of the entrance hall. Walk on towards place Flagey and turn left on avenue Vilain XIIII. At No. 9 and 11 you'll see two more houses built by Blérot in 1902 that are worth mentioning for their sgraffiti, stained-glass windows and artful use of wrought iron.

Next, take a right on rue du Lac to arrive at No. 6. Built in 1904 by Léon Delune, the façade of this house has a surprising geometric originality. Note the play on the architect's surname: the moon in its various phases – full, half, and crescent – can be seen on the façade. The stained-glass window is the work of Raphaël Evaldre.

Vilain XIIII (14)

Avenue Vilain XIIII owes its bizarre numeral (XIIII rather than XIV) to Viscount Charles Hippolyte Vilain XIIII, the former Belgian minister of Foreign Affairs who gave his name to this street. During the siege of Namur (1692–95), one of his ancestors, Jean-Philippe de Vilain, is said to have received permission from the French monarch Louis XIV to add the number fourteen to his name, but only on the express condition of writing it 'XIIII'.

CHILDREN'S MUSEUM

'I see and I forget, I hear and I remember, I do and I understand'

Rue du Bourgmestre 15 – 02 640 01 07
museedesenfants.be – childrenmuseum.brussels@skynet.be
Wednesdays, Saturdays, Sundays and school holidays, 2.30pm–5pm; School groups weekdays by arrangement
Trams No. 90, Chaussée de Boondael stop and No. 80, Place Flagey stop

The Children's Museum is a small corner of heaven for children. More than a museum, it is above all a lively and truly interactive place. Opened over 30 years ago at the initiative of Cathy Van der Straeten and Kathleen Lippens, who discovered the concept in the US city of Boston, this establishment was a forerunner of its kind in Europe. The museum

functions on the basis of temporary but fairly long-running exhibitions that always adhere to the broad theme of self-knowledge through exchanges and communication between the museum coordinators and the children. These exchanges take place during five or six different workshops which require active participation on the part of the children, in accordance with the Chinese proverb: *'I see and I forget, I hear and I remember, I do and I understand.'*

The workshops, each of which is directed by a coordinator, are extremely varied and allow children to take on different roles such as being a tram driver, a raft pilot, a theatre actor, a pastry cook, or a TV reporter and, in short, learn while having fun. The museum is located in a very beautiful townhouse. Built in 1901 in a neo-Louis XV style for the hat-maker Edmond Canonne, in 1923 the property passed into the hands of Lambert Jadot, the brother of Jean Jadot, who was one of the great pioneers of railway construction in China, Egypt, and the Belgian Congo. Bought by the local commune in 1967, this building has housed the museum since 1986. On fine days you can enjoy a drink or a waffle on the sunny terrace. The garden that surrounds the house, named the Parc Jadot, is open to the public throughout the year, and of course offers numerous play facilities for children.

NEARBY
The remains at the Jardins de la Couronne
Avenue de la Couronne – Avenue Auguste-Rodin 8 – Rue Adolphe-Mathieu 1
Bus No. 95, Rodin stop

Covering an area of 6 hectares, the Jardins de la Couronne occupy the former site of the Ixelles Military Hospital. Of the prestigious main building that used to extend 244 metres along avenue de la Couronne, only the corner pavilions formerly occupied by the senior physician and his team still remain. All the other buildings within this large complex have been destroyed after lying abandoned for more than twenty-five years. Today, they have been replaced by the offices lining avenue de la Couronne and a large residential scheme behind it. Walking in the pleasant public park that sits in the centre of the apartment blocks, the visitor is confronted with remains that seem to come straight out of antiquity. Since the hospital was built in a neoclassical style typical of the second half of the 19th century, it had many classical features (columns, porticos, pediments, railings, etc.). Walking around the park, these archaeological remains can be found randomly, whether in a bush or in some hidden corner. The centrepiece of this little open-air museum is an imposing bluestone pediment bearing a Latin inscription: 'Domus mea domus orationis', which translates as 'My house is a house of prayer.' It comes from the old chapel of the military hospital.

MUSEUM OF ZOOLOGY (ULB)

*Driving from Antwerp to Brussels with a lion
as passenger*

ULB Campus du Solbosch Avenue Franklin Roosevelt 50
Bâtiment U, door B (entrance: Square Servais), level 1 (basement), room UAL–319
02 650 36 78 – ulb.ac.be/musees
Monday to Friday, 1pm–5pm (In summer, phone before visiting)
Free individual visit
Guided tour (1 h 30), minimum 10 people
Bus No. 71 or tram No. 94

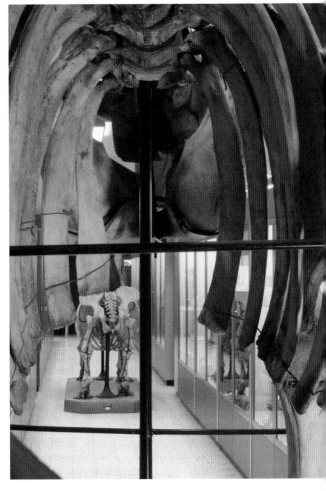

Although not easy to find in the midst of the campus of the Université Libre de Bruxelles, the Musée de Zoologie is worth a visit to see its collection of over 3,000 items. The guided tour, which provides numerous fascinating anecdotes, is recommended.

Your guide will notably expound on the problems of classifying species, which changes over time and in the light of new scientific discoveries. Although the exhibits are displayed by order of growing complexity, Madame Desmet, the curator, fears anthropocentrism and insists: 'It's not because man is part of the most complex system that he is also the most highly evolved or superior creature!'

This sets the tone for a visit that questions many of our assumptions: you learn that, according to DNA analysis, a type of large shrew is a close relative of the elephant, and crocodiles are classified with birds as archosaurs.

Due to their complexity and their biological scarcity, however, some animals defy any attempt at rigorous classification: the duck-billed platypus and the spiny anteater, for example, are classified as mammals but lay eggs like reptiles.

The dentition of animals is also a valuable source of information: the reason rabbits cannot stop gnawing is because this is the only way for these duplicident animals (i.e. having two pairs of incisors in the upper jaw) to keep their teeth from lengthening and curling indefinitely, which would eventually prevent them from eating at all. The teeth of elephants also grow continuously, but only for about 65 years. Once they start to exceed that age and become toothless, they die of starvation.

The star of the show, however, is the coelacanth, a creature that lived 350 million years ago and was once believed to be extinct. But a living specimen was fished from the sea as recently as the 1980s and is found preserved here in an aquarium filled with alcohol. Possessing both gills and lungs, its fleshy fins contain bones similar to our arms and legs, while its manner of swimming resembles walking.

Many of the animals presented here were purchased from Antwerp Zoo. The previous curator has a vivid memory of returning to Brussels by car with a lion as passenger: it wouldn't fit into the boot of his car!

THE TOMB OF
GENERAL BOULANGER

'He died like he lived, as a second lieutenant'

Ixelles Cemetery – Chaussée de Boondael 478, avenue 3
Daily, 9am–4.30pm
Bus No. 71, 72 and 95, Cimetière d'Ixelles stop

Cemeteries, veritable miniature cities, have their share of the extraordinary and of small and great men. Ixelles cemetery is a fascinating example. When you enter, ask the attendant for the leaflet that presents the celebrities buried here: Antoine Wiertz, Ernest Solvay, Victor Horta, Camille Lemonnier, Charles De Coster, Marcel Broothaers and Paul Nougé, to name but a few. Of all of them, the man with the most astonishing fate and surprising death is undeniably General Boulanger.

This French officer and politician, born in 1837 in Rennes, is known for having shaken the Third Republic as the impetus of the 'Boulangist movement, a strange synthesis of burgeoning Socialism and vengeful nationalism against Germany. As director of the infantry, Boulanger first became popular for his numerous reforms. They were trivial reforms meant to please the infantrymen, such as adding cod to the rations and authorizing non-commissioned officers to wear a beard. When he became War Minister in 1886, he continued along the same lines, notably by replacing the mess tins with plates and the straw mattresses with spring mattresses, authorizing the men to have their own forks or by eliminating the military service exemption for parish priests. In 1889, he relinquished the idea of committing a coup d'état, but the government accused him of plotting against state security. He had no choice but to take refuge in Brussels with his mistress, Marguerite

de Bonnemains. On 15 July 1891 she died of tuberculosis. Georges Boulanger committed suicide two and a half months later by shooting himself at the grave of his beloved in Ixelles Cemetery.

A broken column symbolizing Marguerite' untimely death indicates the location of the grave. The plaque denoting the full identities of the deceased couple has been stolen. All that remains is this dialogue engraved in the stone: 'Marguerite, I'll see you soon / Georges, how could I have lived two and a half months without you.' It clear why Brussels Surrealists adore this site and organize ceremonies in memory of this love-stricken general. Georges Clémenceau, however, was less enthusiastic about the romantic death of his former schoolmate. When he learned of his suicide, he laconically retorted, 'He died like he lived, as a second lieutenant.'

NEARBY
Brussels' first 'listed tree'

According to legend, Charles V himself stopped in front of the lime tree situated behind the Boondael Chapel before joining the nocturnal hunting parties in the Sonian Forest (Forêt de Soignes). This very old lime tree, planted around the beginning of the 17th century, is in fact 'only' 400 years old. Its great age and the fact that it is completely hollow at its roots have led to it being reinforced with metal hoops and concrete. In 1936 it became the first tree in Brussels to be listed.

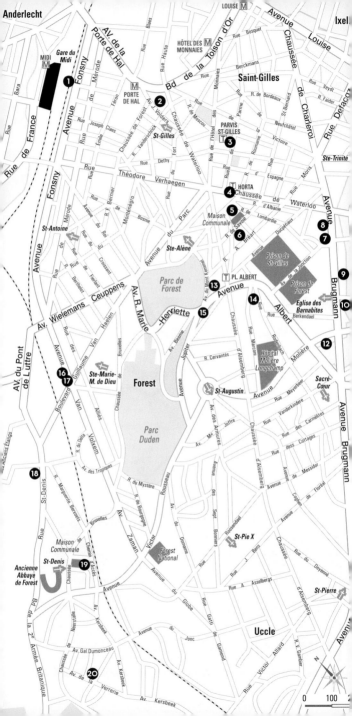

Saint-Gilles and Forest

PATERNOSTER LIFT OF THE SNCB ①

The lift that doesn't stop at the top floor ...

Avenue Fonsny 47B
Access Gare du Midi

A long the mysterious corridors of power and bureaucracy, the authorities sometimes reveal hidden treasures! Such is the case of the Société Nationale des Chemins de Fer Belges premises, where you can take a vertical trip that's really out of the ordinary.

Here there's still an example of a paternoster lift, an elevator in perpetual motion that never stops at any floor. The principle is simple: no doors, no stops, you just take the lift 'on the fly', right cabin to go up, left cabin to go down. Your first, theoretic, reaction, is pleasure at not having to wait long minutes wondering what's going on a few floors above. In practice it can be rather more disconcerting.

Although it runs slowly, it's better that way, as some people are uncomfortable with this mechanism developed some 50 years ago. Yet it's true that you shouldn't be too slow in getting in when the lift goes by, if not you'll have to wait until it comes round again. Inside, a notice tries to reassure the anxious user: '*La traversée du grenier et de la cave est sans danger*' (There is no danger when the lift crosses the top floor and the ground floor).

But let's not exaggerate. Once the initial surprise has passed, all goes well. For security reasons, nevertheless, the lift is banned to children and disabled people.

Although these lifts are only found today in a few venerable institutions, they used to be very popular as, at 15 cm a second, they were faster than escalators. Today, the cabins of the Mitsubishi lift at Yokohama turn at 45 km an hour.

When you visit, ask the caretaker nicely to let you try the lift.

Why 'paternoster'?
The name of this mythical lift comes from the appearance of the of the system: the movement of the cabins, suspended from two chains driven by toothed pulleys, evokes the dozens of beads of the rosary as you recite the Lord's Prayer (*Pater Noster* in Latin).

ART NOUVEAU ENSEMBLE ON RUE VANDERSCHRICK

②

Blérot gems

Rue Vanderschrick 1–25
Chaussée de Waterloo 13–15
Rue Jean Volders 42–48

© Rebecho

onstructed between 1900 and 1903 by Ernest Blérot, the rue Vanderschrick ensemble was listed in 1988. It is the only example in Brussels of Art Nouveau executed on such a scale: 16 adjoining houses, the total length of a street.

It owes its existence to the decision of the commune in 1898 to extend rue Vanderschrick, creating a new link between rue de l'Église and chaussée de Waterloo.

The widow Elsom acquired one side completely and had it built on two years later. No. 1 to 13 (first phase) are differentiated from No. 15 to 25 (second phase) by their commercial ground floors. Tastefully restored, this ensemble has definite charm.

The sgraffiti take up Blérot's favourite themes: sunrise, sunset, and other less frequent ones such as ponds with water lilies or birds against a blue sky.

The restaurant at No. 25 is a neo-Art Nouveau creation of the 1990s with a painful lack of charm, unless you count the original toilets.

Also built by Blérot, 13 chaussée de Waterloo offers attractive sgraffiti, as do the buildings between 42 and 48 avenue Jean Volders.

Ernest Blérot (Bruxelles 1870 – Elzenwalle (Ypres) 1957)

Next to Victor Horta, Blérot was the most appreciated architect in Brussels at the beginning of the 20th century. Far from possessing the genius of his colleague who gave a whole new conception to architecture, Blérot remained a master of decorative art.

Using a single standardized plan, with no real architectural concern, he concentrated his energy on decorating façades, for which veritable individual work was carried out. This standardization allowed him to lower both the timescale and the costs of production, which appealed more to petite bourgeoise clients for whom the aesthetic effect of the façade was more important than interior comforts.

In around a decade, Blérot built some 60 houses in Brussels including three remarkable groups: Vanderschrik at Saint-Gilles (17 homes side by side), in the Saint-Boniface district of Ixelles where there are 11 of his buildings; and at Les Etangs d'Ixelles, also with 11.

Sgraffiti

A vast number of sgraffiti now decorate the façades of Brussels houses and buildings. Most of them owe their existence to the development of Art Nouveau which used this very ancient technique with great abandon, though not exclusively. Derived from the Italian *sgraffiare* (to scratch away), the term *sgraffito* describes a technique of wall decoration that involves covering a surface with a thin coat of plaster then scratching the design in the damp material to expose the layer below.

Often carried out in two colours (white and silver-grey) in the Italian Renaissance, notably by the painter and architect Giorgio Vasari, sgraffiti was rediscovered in the 19th century in Western Europe under the influence of the Neo-Renaissance architect and writer Gottfried Semper (1803–79).

Originally in one or two colours, sgraffiti then developed further and the technique was refined: engraved lines were used as well as simply scratching the surface, and the use of colour grew.

Grey, dark green or brown took over from black as background colour. The covering wash evolved from plain chalk-white to a yellower tone. Finally, a fresco painting technique (tinting the mortar while still wet) was used to give a richer palette of colours and more depth to the design.

In Brussels, the first major project decorated with sgraffiti that can still be seen is probably Hôtel Goblet d'Alviella, 10 rue Faider, Saint-Gilles, built in 1882. But the construction of the private home of Paul Hankar, at 71 rue Defacqz, marked a turning point. Setting a benchmark for sgraffiti in the years to come, the building also gradually asserted itself as a major achievement of Art Nouveau. Without really being aware of it, architect Paul Hankar and decorator Adolphe Crespin here laid the groundwork for a fruitful collaboration For many Brussels residents, Art Nouveau and sgraffiti have become almost indivisible. Only Victor Horta and Paul Vizzavona refused to use sgraffiti to decorate the façades of their Art Nouveau buildings.

In Brussels, the great architects who expressed themselves in sgraffiti were Crespin (notably 48 and 71 rue Defacqz, 26 rue de Parme), Henri Baes (12 rue Van Moer), Privat Livemont (17 rue Vogler, 6 place des Bienfaiteurs, 16 rue Locquenghien, 83 rue Faider, 58 rue des Capucins, school complexes 229 rue Josaphat and 103 rue Roodebeek), Paul Cauchie (notably 5 rue des Francs, 47 rue Malibran, 297 avenue d'Auderghem), Gabriel Van Divoet or even Ernest Blérot and Gustave Strauven.

PELGRIMS HOUSE

*Art Deco and Renaissance: a fine example
of eclectic architecture*

*Rue de Parme 69
02 534 56 05
Metro Hôtel des Monnaies*

Maison Pelgrims is unique in Saint-Gilles: a vast townhouse alone in a park that used to be its private garden. There are two ways of visiting it nowadays. The first is to meekly wait for one of the (regular) organized events: concerts, opening nights, etc. Stay in touch with the various municipal publications or ring for information. The other method is simply to ring the bell marked 'Service de la culture'. The Cultural Services have been installed here since 2001 when the community hall became too cramped. If you ask nicely and if the staff have time, they'll be pleased to open the door for you and show you round the most interesting rooms of the house. As it isn't officially open to the public on a regular basis, they'll be doing this as a favour, so appreciate this and understand that sometimes they may have to refuse to let people in.

Acquired by the commune in 1963 and listed in June 2001, the Pelgrims house is a fine example of the eclectic style that marked Brussels at the close of the 19th century. While the superb winter garden announces Art Deco with its blue-tinted glass, fountain and mosaics, the loggia on the ground floor overlooking the garden has links with the Italian architecture of Renaissance villas. Built in 1905 by the architect Adolphe Pirenne for the Colson family, the house was bought by the wealthy pharmacist Pelgrims in 1927, who then asked the architect Fernand Petit to make some alterations. Some 10 years later, Petit made a name for himself with the construction of the Gare du Midi and the Régie des Postes.

The building enjoys an exceptional location overlooking the park, most of which is the former garden of Notre-Dame-du-Cénacle convent. Laid out as a country park in the English fashion, the garden possesses a lake fed by the Elsbeek, one of the last vestiges of the sources of Saint-Gilles water. Fake ruins making reference to antiquity and the passing of time give the place a certain charm.

The park, known as Pierre Paulus in honour of the painter and engraver who was the first president of the Saint-Gilles art group, was listed in 1997.

SGRAFFITI ON CHAUSSÉE DE WATERLOO

When the sun meets the moon

Chaussée de Waterloo 246–256

Built in 1901 by the architect Jean-Pierre Van Oostveen, the si
houses between numbers 246 and 256 Chaussée de Waterlo
feature a few architectural gems.

Was it out of modesty that he signed only one stone? Or was
because he was not among the best-known architects of the Brussels A.
Nouveau movement?

The most beautiful house is at number 250. Recently restored, it h

a beautifully balanced façade. A frieze supports the two windows that are themselves topped by seven small bays decorated with magnificent stained glass in geometric shapes. The upper balcony is topped with a magnificent sgraffito depicting the day and the night.

This sgraffito, like the entire façade, was covered in white paint at a time, not so long ago, when Art Nouveau was no longer popular.

Some of Brussels' magnificent and exuberant works – by Victor Horta, Ernest Blérot and Paul Hankar, to name but a few – have been irretrievably destroyed, replaced with the banal constructions of property developers from the 1960s. Only the house at No. 254 has kept its original ground floor and a beautiful door. The fronts of the other five houses were converted into shop windows between 1930 and 1950.

TOWN HALL OF SAINT-GILLES ⑤

Built in the style of a Renaissance palace,
the Hôtel de Ville was decorated by over 107 artists

Place Van Meenen 39
02 536 02 11
Guided tour by arrangement
Trams No. 81 and 82, Horta stop

© Jean-Jacques Evrard

I t's too often forgotten that the Saint-Gilles Hôtel de Ville is a veritable mini-museum of early 20th-century art. Its administrative function means that by definition it's open to the public, thus visits are free.

Responding to a constantly growing population and an initiative on the part of bourgmestre Van Meenen, who later lent his name to the town square, the Hôtel de Ville was inaugurated in 1904. With its 42 m bell tower, it was built in the style of a Renaissance palace by the self-taught architect Albert Dumont (1853-1920), responsible for the planning of De Panne on the Belgian coast in 1895 and Hardelot-Plage in France. Over 107 artists contributed to the decoration of the building, in accordance with the wishes of the community council.

There are a number of statues gracing the exterior. In the entrance to the *Cour d'Honneur* stands a Jef Lambeaux sculpture *La Désse du Bocq (The Goddess of Bocq)*, which caused a sensation when it was installed. Intended to symbolize the bringing of piped water from the Bocq River, the sculpture of a young, willowy-limbed nude offended the public, as had *Passions Humaines* in the Horta pavilion at the Parc du Cinquantenaire (see p. 118), and so it disappeared into the cellars. The statue was only put back in place in 1976.

The interior is equally remarkable and most of the rooms are accessible: you only need to open the door. The great hall and staircase are decorated with several panels by Cluysenaar father and son, Jacques de Lalaing and Albert Ciamberlani, as well as a Carrera marble statue by Jef Lambeaux, *La Volupté (Voluptuousness)*, and the original version of *La Porteuse d'Eau (The Water Carrier)* by Julien Dillens. A symbol of the commune, the latter is inspired by a young girl who used to water the horses that drew the omnibus along chaussée de Waterloo as far as La Barrière, where a copy of the famous statue now stands.

The registry office has a beautiful ceiling painted by Fernand Khnopff, as well as tapestries by Hélène de Rudder. Nearby you'll see a fine collection of antique pottery. The most sumptuous chamber is probably the Salle des Pas Perdus, decorated by Omer Dierickx who took over four years to finish the ceiling composition *La Liberté descendant sur le monde aux acclamations de l'Humanité (Liberty Descending on the World to the Acclamations of Humanity)*.

ART NOUVEAU WALK IN SAINT-GILLES

One of the most remarkable Art Nouveau ensembles in Brussels

Avenue Jef Lambeaux 12, 35, 36 and 38 – Avenue Paul Dejaer 9
Chaussée de Waterloo 246, 248 and 250 – Rue Antoine Bréart 7
Rue M. Wilmotte 28 – Place Louis Morichar 14 et 41
Rue de Parme 26 – Rue de l'Hôtel des Monnaies 66 – Rue Vanderschrick
Metro Porte de Hal, trams No. 3, 55 and 92, Horta stop

Although Saint-Gilles has a rich architectural Art Nouveau heritage, the buildings can sometimes be of limited interest to the non-specialist. We thus propose a walk to discover the most interesting Art Nouveau façades in the neighbourhood. We'll begin at avenue Jef Lambeaux, No. 38, with an attractive and little known sgraffito. Just next door is No. 36, a fine house built in 1900 (architect A. Malchair).

© Jean-Jacques Evrard

Opposite, No. 35, was built by Cl. Verhas in 1910. Finally, still in the same street, No. 12 was built by Georges Peereboom for Antoine Peereboom, an expert surveyor and politician representing Saint-Gilles in 1898. Continue down avenue Jef Lambeaux in the direction of rue de Savoie.

Turn left and after a while stop for a beer at Moeder Lambic, a well-known local bar that opens around four in the afternoon. Turn right alongside the Hôtel de Ville. In place Van Meenen, take rue Paul Dejaer in front of you. At No. 9 you'll see a superb house by G. Strauven dating from 1901. When you come to La Barrière, take chaussée de Waterloo on the right where at No. 246, 248 and 250 you'll see three beautiful houses built in 1905 by J.P. Van Oostveen. The following houses, from No. 252 to No. 256, are less spectacular examples by the same architect. A little further on, take the third street on the right. Just at the corner, No. 7 rue Antoine Bréart was built in 1898 by Paul Hankar for the tailor Jean-Baptiste Aglave (pretty sgraffiti by Adolphe Crespin). Retrace your steps along chaussée de Waterloo. Left then first right, No. 28 rue M. Wilmotte is a fine construction by A. Toisoul. Note the large sgraffito of a seated woman. Stroll back the way you came and take rue d'Espagne on the right. You'll soon reach place Louis Morichar where, at No. 41, you'll find a magnificent house constructed in 1900 by Blérot.

The mosaics are particularly admirable, remarkable for their colour and originality. Opposite, on the other side of the square stands No. 14, the very fine Delcoigne house, decorated with attractive sgraffiti and built in 1899 by Georges Delcoigne. Next cross the square, turning right into rue du Lycée which shortly runs into rue de Parme. There is a former photographic studio at No. 26. Built in 1897 by Fernand Symons, it has pretty sgraffiti carried out by Adolphe Crespin. Go back a few steps and turn right into rue de la Victoire then right again into rue de l'Hôtel des Monnaies. At No. 66 is Horta's Hôtel Winssinger (see p. 84).

If by any chance you should feel the need for a haircut, now's your chance. Almost opposite, at No. 81, is the 'Salon d'Art', one of the most original and pleasant hairdressing salons in the city. Finally, take rue de la Victoire towards Porte de Hal. Third on the right, finish this walk in the beauty of rue Vandreschrick with one of the most remarkable Art Nouveau ensembles in Brussels (see p. 164). You can if you wish prolong your walk by adding Hôtel Hannon, 1 rue de la Jonction and Les Hiboux House (see p. 177), followed by the celebrated Horta Museum at 23–25 rue Américaine (not covered in this guide), and lastly rue Defacqz to admire three works by Paul Hankar (see p. 140).

MAISON HANNON

The only Art Nouveau work by the architect Jules Brunfaut

Avenue de la Jonction 1
Wednesday and Friday 11am–6pm and weekends 1pm–6pm
Booking: maisonhannon.be

Today occupied by the photographic association Contretype, the magnificent Hôtel Hannon is one of the finest examples of Art Nouveau in Brussels. Built in 1902 by the architect Jules Brunfaut, this townhouse has the remarkable attribute of being his only work in the Art Nouveau style. He was actually a close friend of the owner, Edouard Hannon, and he expressed his friendship in trying out a new style for him in this building.

The result speaks volumes. Clearly inspired by Horta, as well as Van

Rysselberghe, Brunfaut also called upon the famous master glassmaker of Nancy, Émile Gallé, for the furnishings and on the Rouen painter Paul Edouard Baudoin, pupil of Puvis de Chavanne, for the superb staircase fresco.

The house was abandoned in 1965 on the death of Denise Hannon, the owner's daughter, and was threatened with demolition by a property developer. The district council rose up against this aberration and the Saint-Gilles commune bought the house in 1976, the year it was listed, although the restoration wasn't complete until 1988.

During this time most of the furnishings disappeared. Some can now be seen at the *Musée des Arts Décoratifs* in Paris. Although the building now serves as a space for photographic exhibitions (a nice gesture to Edouard Hannon's passion for photography), it is particularly valued for its exterior architecture and its ground floor, staircase and fresco.

A home, not a hotel

Although it was listed in 1976 as Hôtel Hannon, the building is now called Maison Hannon, because it has none of the architectural features that would make it a mansion: no vestibule or carriage entrance, no service staircase for the servants, no kitchen cellar or maids' rooms, and a relatively narrow façade.

For the sake of accuracy and respect for the intentions of the Hannons, it was decided to rename this residence Maison Hannon because, although large and luxurious, it was above all the living quarters of two connoisseurs and by no means intended as a stately home.

NEARBY
Les Hiboux House   (8)
Avenue Brugmann 55
Another beautiful example of an Art Nouveau house in Brussels, built in 1895 by Edouard Pelseneer (1870–1947). Note the sgraffiti of the two owls for whom the house is named, as well as the round windows that give the impression of looking fixedly at you, like owls' eyes. The house is privately owned.

Fernand Dubois House   (9)
Avenue Brugmann 80
This is the former house of the sculptor Fernand Dubois, built between 1901 and 1903 by Victor Horta, although this is not his most spectacular or most accomplished work.

HOUSE AND STUDIO
OF LOUISE DE HEM

Stunning sgraffito of a world-renowned artist

Rue Darwin 15 and 17

At the beginning of the 20th century, the sculptor and painter Louise De Hem, known worldwide for her portrait paintings, had the architect Ernest Blérot build her studio at No. 17 (1902) and her house at No. 15 (1905), although some believe she designed the studio façade herself.

The wide, floral, Art Nouveau façade of the studio features a superb sgraffito depicting the artist at work. The narrower façade of the house is more ornate, with two very fine sgraffiti depicting a cockerel at sunrise and, above it, four swallows in flight.

An almost exact copy of this house, in terms of architecture and decoration, can be found on Place Morichar 41 in Saint Gilles. It was also built by Ernest Blérot.

Hôtel Philippot ⑪
Avenue Molière 153–155
Built by the architect Jules Brunfaut (also responsible for Hôtel Hannon) in 1908, the majesty of the façade is impressive as is the large bas-relief by Jef Lambeaux. You can also admire the luminous owls at No. 151.

Avenue Molière 172 ⑫
Beautiful mosaics representing eagles and stylized motifs with an Egyptian influence decorate the façade of No. 172. The architect Jean-Baptiste Dewin often applied this decorative technique.

NELISSEN HOUSE

A breathtaking circular bay

Avenue du Mont Kemmel 5
Forest

© Jean-Jacques Evrard

Built just opposite Forest's park, the personal home of architect Arthur Nelissen, also known as Villa Beau-Site, is a spectacular Art Nouveau building from 1905.

Its most striking feature is the huge circular bay that cuts the façade in two on the first floor, which is a typical geometric feature characteristic of the Art Nouveau style.

Arthur Nelissen was an eclectic Dutch architect mainly active in Brussels. Built for his personal use, the house was intended to demonstrate his qualities as a contemporary architect.

Black and white glazed bricks around the circular bay are reminiscent of the keys of a piano.

NEARBY

Cité Mosselmans ⑭
Rue Marconi 32

At No. 32 rue Marconi, the Mosselmans housing estate boasts a spectacular Egyptian-inspired smooth concrete and cement entrance porch of Egyptian inspiration, designed by architect Léon Govaerts between 1901 and 1903. In the same street, at Nos. 34 to 42, four other buildings are remarkable for the diversity of their styles and their excellent state of preservation. Meant for social housing, each was designed by a different architect. In neighbouring rue Rodenbach (Nos. 14 to 31), don't miss a remarkable eclectic-style estate in yellow and red brick and bluestone, comprising two large identical buildings facing each other.

Villa De Rooster ⑮
Avenue Besme 103

Built in 1903 for Mr De Rooster by the architect Alphonse Boelens (1877–1936), the Villa De Rooster is a remarkable Art Nouveau-style building with three façades. The façade on the avenue side is typical of this period with its rounded window surrounded by beautiful cut stone, window panelling and balconies and matching ironwork, all in a fairly geometric style. Numerous sgraffiti decorate it. The current owners, under the supervision of Monuments et Sites, have carried out major restoration work that has restored the villa to its former splendour.

THE FOXES ON VAN VOLXEM AVENUE

The foxes, ducks and the little mouse

Avenue Van Volxem 268 and 270

Built in 1895 by a little-known architect called Edgard Fouarge, the two almost twin neighbouring houses on Avenue Van Volxem, Nos. 268 and 270, are typical of the Brussels Art Nouveau style: a mix of yellow brick and blue stone, elaborate plant forms in the wrought ironwork, rectangular window frames that blend elegantly into the circular masonry, basement windows and lower sections cut in a semicircle.

What really sets these two houses apart is the animal decoration.

The balcony of the house on the right, at No. 270, is supported by two grey foxes.

There is a little mouse that seems to be trying to escape on the handles of the two entrance doors, the doorbell at No. 268 features a duck's head, and the postman can slide the mail into the beak of another duck in the letterbox of the same house.

Avenue Van Volxem was built in 1874 on land that was planted with trees and farmland. Did the architect want to pay tribute to the animals that lived there?

THE DOOR AT NO. 317 AVENUE VAN VOLXEM ⑰

The gateway to paradise

Avenue Van Volxem 317

L ocated just opposite the foxes on Avenue Van Volxem (see previous page), on the opposite side of the road, the house at No. 317 has a magnificent and discreet front door.

The door is a masterpiece of typically Art Deco wrought iron, made up of scrolls and stylised flowers and, at its centre, a sort of bird of paradise flying into the sunset. Above, the awning that bears the name of the ironmonger who lived there acts as a sort of visiting card for his business.

AUDI BRUSSELS

*A 50 hectare car factory only 15 minutes
from the city centre*

Boulevard de la Deuxième Armée Britannique 201
02 348 26 46 – visit.audibx@audi.de
Tours by arrangement
Trams No. 18 and 52

Brussels is probably the only European capital to possess a major factory scarcely 15 minutes from the city centre. Extending over more than 50 hectares, the factory will surprise the uninitiated by the sheer size of the various buildings. Some of them are as much as 200 m long and 60 m high, such as the paint shop, which is closed to the public for security reasons.

Not forgetting that it has some potential clients in the audience, Audi Brussels begins the tour with a short film praising the qualities of the group and its different makes of vehicle. Then you head for the immense halls where the various pressed-steel body panels delivered from the mother factory in Wolfsburg, Germany, are assembled. The ballet begins, in a web of empty carcasses of vehicles, robots, travelling cranes and assembly lines. You begin to see the complexity of the path followed by a car through the factory, turning, rising, turning again to undergo another treatment in the gaunt arms of a new-generation robot. The lack of human presence in the factory, which is over 90% automated, fires your imagination. Yet it employs more than 5,000 people.

Once the panel assembly is finished, we move on to fittings. The car, still a metallic skeleton, is thus equipped with engine, wheels, dashboard and various indispensable accessories before undergoing its final inspection.

Despite the obvious size of the site, the facilities are now rather cramped and the central location doesn't allow for the expansion that would help the company to resolve its organizational problems and compete effectively. For this reason, Volkswagen had planned to close the factory a few years ago. Meanwhile, Renault closed its Vilvorde plant ... the ensuing clamour of protest forced the directors to abandon their project.

STAINED GLASS WINDOWS
OF THE FOREST

The finest Art Deco stained glass in the city

Rue du Curé 2
Trams No. 18 and 52, Forest-Centre stop

Opposite the abbey, the Forest community hall is a fine Art Deco building by Jean-Baptiste Dewin, dating from 1934. If most of its visitors are there only for administrative reasons, the building deserves a tour on its own merits, to admire the richness of its architecture and interior decoration. A visit is so much easier when it's free during normal opening hours.

Going in from the abbey courtyard side, immediately to the left in the Salle des Pas Perdus, note the stained glass created in 1939 by the master glassmaker Colpaert after designs by Balthus. Climb the grand staircase in front of you. Other stained-glass windows are signed by the same artists.

The different rooms, in a very pure Art Deco style, are worth a detour. Note the rich materials used to decorate the interior, exotic woods and marbles, as well as the bronze sculptures by Minne and Verbeyst.

Outside there is an attractive belfry reminiscent of the Middle Ages, ornamentation praising the virtues of family life and sculptures by Victor Rousseau.

FOREST VERT ESTATE

*Cité Forest-Vert, between town and country,
is a paradise for the curious rambler*

Around avenue de Fléron
Trams No. 18 and 52

The district lying between rue du Général Dumonceau, rue de la Verrerie and rue de Fleron in Forest is a remarkable tangle of narrow little passages with a rural air about them, where the plants have sometimes taken over. At the border between town and country, the Forest Vert Estate is a paradise for the curious and sharp-eyed rambler, as the entrances to this labyrinth of paths and garden plots are not always easy to spot.

There are two blocks of housing here, on either side of rue de Fleron. The odd-numbered, and larger, side is the more charming and intriguing. No less than 14 entrances lead to what the residents call the Plaine Centrale, a superb little green space with a lawn and five benches that can only be reached on foot. What a pleasure to sit down for a moment, read the newspaper and watch the local children criss-crossing the paths. A woman is at her window, she calls over to a man coming out of his garden with his lawnmower. A mother pushes her son in his stroller. Watch out in the evening, however, as a rather different population will be up to other things.

The entrances are to the left of No. 51, 63, 69, 75 and 83 of rue du Général Dumonceau, and to the right of No. 63 in the same street. Other entrances lie on each side of the end of square de Glasblazerij (rue de la Verrerie between No. 42 and 94), left of No. 98 rue de la Verrerie and No. 45 avenue de Fleron, right of No. 25 and 37 avenue de Fleron and rue des Bonnes Mères, at the rear corner of the only building in the street.

A similar group of alleyways is to be found on the other side of rue de Fleron, entrances to the left of No. 64 and right of No. 72 rue de Fleron, left of No. 120 and right of No. 128 avenue de la Verrerie, opposite No. 2–3 avenue des Familles and at the corner of rue de Fleron and avenue de la Verrerie, on the even-numbered side. This block is less spacious and pleasant than the other, much of it now being taken up with the annex to the École des Tilleuls.

The Forest Vert Estate, a garden city built in 1922 by the architect Henri Montfort, was partly demolished in the 1950s to make way for a housing project on this side of rue de Fleron. Despite that, the city's houses with gardens have over the years become desirable residences.

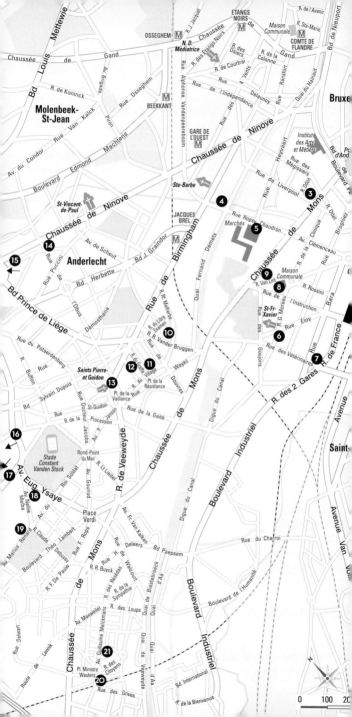

Anderlecht

SEWER MUSEUM

Under the streets of Brussels, 2 million rats eat a third of the waste

Pavillon de l'Octroi – Porte d'Anderlecht
02 279 60 32
sewermuseum.brussels
Daily, 10am–5pm, open by arrangement for groups, with guided tour Thursdays and Fridays
Trams No. 18, 46 and 82, Porte d'Anderlecht stop

Not given the recognition it deserves, the Sewer Museum offers by arrangement an interesting guided tour of the local sewers. You can visit historic and technical installations on three levels, as well as accessing the actual sewer network. One particular feature is that the guides work in the network itself, so you're dealing here with real experts who know what they're talking about.

Historically, the sewer system once consisted of a single open-air channel running down the middle of the street, hence the French expression *tenir le haut du pavé*, meaning 'to be at the top' (of the pavement), where the sewage did not run. Today, the Brussels network comprises 300 km of underground sewers, thousands of related installations that gather the waste water (from kitchens and bathrooms, for example), and 30 km of collecteurs. These are bigger than classic sewers, and as their name indicates they collect water from the rest of the network for final waste treatment.

They are cleaned by wagons-vans, one of which is on display in the second chamber visited during the guided tour, specially built to fit the collector's dimensions.

But there is another sewer cleaning agent: the rat. There are no less than two million rats living beneath the surface of Brussels, about two for each of the city's human residents! On their own, they manage to eat about a third of the waste present in the sewers. To be sure, finding yourself face-to-face with a 50 cm specimen is distasteful (to say the least!), but the 60-odd employees of the municipal sewer service are used to them and not in the least frightened. All the more so because, contrary to common opinion, the rats don't live in the sewers, they only use them to move around, spending most of their time just beneath our feet, in the nooks and crannies of the domestic water drains or under people's cellars.

The tour ends with a journey through the modern network. You first visit one of the vaulted channels of the Senne that runs underneath the museum and from there you go to the collector for the sewers in the chaussée de Mons. Surprisingly, the sewer network is in fact linked with the Senne river as it passes beneath the city. Running in a vaulted tunnel in the centre of Brussels since 1863, the river acts as a safety valve for the sewer system in case of flooding. If this were not so, the sewers might overflow on days of heavy rain, and in that case, the only outlet would be the streets themselves. The manhole covers would lift from the pressure of the rising waters of filth.

Although today certain people cherish the dream of returning the Senne to the open air in some sections, which might be charming, of course, this would require two major changes: cleaning up the river waters, and building or finding another means of drainage in case of flooding.

One last detail, if you book a tour, you might like to know that the Cureghem abattoir kills animals on Tuesdays and Thursdays. On those two days of the week, the sewer waters beneath the museum take on an astonishing blood-red hue.

NEARBY

Former headquarters of Prévoyance Sociale ②

Square de l'Aviation 29
CEGES reading room (02 556 92 11) is open Monday to Friday 9am–12pm and 1pm–5pm

Although this handsome Art Deco building is not officially open to the public, it's nevertheless worthwhile turning up at CEGES (Centre d'Études et de Documentation, Guerre et Sociétés Contemporaines) which has its offices here: their reading room, which is open to the public, is located on the mezzanine and gives an ideal view of the paquebot style of architecture (the rounded forms and rails recalling the great ocean liners) in the hall with the former information counters for the public, magnificently preserved.

Today this space houses an impressive archive of documents concerning

© Jean-Jacques Evrard

the political, economic, social and cultural crises and conflicts that marked the history of the 20th century.

The glass cupola that surmounts the building and the archives tower can be visited during the *journées du patrimoine* (open-door heritage days).

School No. 8 ③

Rue Abbé Cuylits 27

In a deprived neighbourhood, École No. 8, which stands between rues Odon and Cuylits, presents a handsome façade on rue Cuylits, decorated with sgraffiti. These represent the various subjects studied in the school: drawing, history, geography, music, writing, reading, geometry, arithmetic, natural sciences (illustrated with a curious skull) and gymnastics. Two other beautiful sgraffiti portraying a woman holding a child by the hand are less well preserved. This school was built in 1897 to plans drawn up by the commune's architect, E. S'Jonghers.

BLACKSMITHING SCHOOL (IEPSCF)

Learn the blacksmith's trade on the hooves of horses slaughtered at Cureghem

Rue Léon Delacroix 28
02 410 26 73
ecoledemarechalerie.be
Open House Weekend generally held the last weekend of April
Metro Delacroix

The light metal roof of the slaughterhouse market has dominated the town of Cureghem since 1888. This veritable city within the city greatly influenced the economy of this area of Anderlecht, from

the large number of butcher's shops and delicatessens, the tanneries and leather goods shops, to the veterinary school, the abandoned buildings of which still stand nearby.

Given this specialized local industry, the Department of Agriculture decided to establish a blacksmithing school here in 1931, just a few dozen metres away from the slaughterhouses. This judicious location allowed trainees to spend the first half of their studies practising on the hooves of slaughtered horses. The street-side façade of this school designed by architect A. J. Storrer is rather eye-catching, thanks to its Art Deco lines, which are stylishly enhanced by woodwork painted in red and a series of blacksmithing tools, such as horseshoes, hammers and anvils.

The building is divided into two schools, one of which is Dutch-speaking and the other French-speaking. In the latter, about 150 Belgian, but also French, trainees (who come to learn the specific smithy techniques taught almost exclusively here) try their hand at the delicate art of shoeing horses. As it is a very difficult, dangerous and physically demanding job, the majority of the trainees are male, but there are several young women in the student body.

During their three years of training, they must learn how to make around 30 different types of horseshoe, from rather simple ones for healthy horses to veritable orthopaedic shoes for injured or disabled horses.

The classes given here essentially provide practical experience, as the main classroom – a large workshop filled with a dozen forges – indicates. This experience is complemented by classes in technology, anatomy, physiology, and the pathologies of horse hooves.

Of course, it is quite understandable that, theoretically, visits aren't allowed, but you can always make a polite request at the entrance to take a glance at the workshop. However, you shouldn't miss the Open House Weekend (generally held the last weekend of April), when this unique school offers tours and blacksmithing demonstrations.

NEARBY

Greenhouses on the roof of the Anderlecht abattoir

(5)

Rue Ropsy Chaudron 24, 1070 Anderlecht – 02 512 03 24

On the site of the Anderlecht slaughterhouse (still in operation today), an amazing farm has been set up on the roof of the Foodmet, the indoor hall of the Anderlecht market. The aquaponic farm grows vegetables, berries and aromatic herbs and rears trout. All the produce is sold in shops in and around Brussels. You can visit the outdoor garden, greenhouses and fishponds while enjoying the breathtaking view over Brussels.

FORGOTTEN FAÇADES OF RUE GEORGES MOREAU

In the street, be careful not to come across the wrong numbers

Rue Georges Moreau 148, 162, 164 and 170
Access Gare du Midi

© Jean-Jacques Evrard

Avenue Georges Moreau has some very beautiful façades off the traditional beaten track in this neighbourhood.

Coming from the direction of the École Vétérinaire, the façade at No. 148 includes a sgraffito, unfortunately in poor condition.

A little further to the right, the former workshop/home of Victor Delplanque, maker of enamelled plaques, was built by architect Arthur Nélissen in 1906. Its façade is decorated with some very pretty enamelled plaques. Note in particular the pictures of a swan and a peacock.

One small unusual feature is that these twin houses are numbered 172 and 174. But as you go along the right-hand side of the avenue, you'll be surprised to see houses numbered 170 and then a second 172! The street numbers of the previous two houses are simply false. Following recent renovation work, for some mysterious reason the owner had them inscribed with the wrong numbers. The real numbers are 162 and 164. The postman is aware of the mix-up so the residents still receive their respective mail.

The most beautiful house in this avenue is certainly the one at No. 170. Built in 1908 by architect and surveyor Hector Gérard, it combines medieval, Renaissance and Art Nouveau influences. In particular it has a magnificent sgraffito in good condition, although the author is unknown. An ode to painting, and in particular, to several Flemish painters, the house was recently restored.

The names of Rogier Van der Weyden, Jan Van der Meeren, Memling, David, Blondeel and Lucas Van Leyden, as well as Hubert and Jan Van Eyck, are all inscribed here. Encircling the pretty wooden bow window on the first floor, the sgraffito represents four women surrounded by garlands of flowers and arabesques.

LAST STRETCH OF THE SENNE BEFORE IT RUNS UNDERGROUND

Shortly afterwards, the river passes below the city

Rue des Vétérinaires
Access Gare du Midi

Right at the start of rue des Vétérinaires, just before the Brussels-Paris railway bridge, is a piece of waste land with a service station and car wash. Between the two, behind a small car park, a lane ascends towards the railway. On the right, alongside the brick building, a little path leads off through the weeds and affords a view of the last open-air section of the Senne River. The verdant environment is misleading because the Senne is far from being clean, despite recent efforts. Upriver, near the Viangros premises, the Bruxelles Sud water purification plant was installed in autumn 2000. But this isn't enough, and a brief glimpse of the river from rue Bollinckx reveals that the water is already quite polluted before it even reaches the Brussels conurbation. To say nothing of its state once it comes out on the far side…

You can still find other traces of the Senne in Brussels. In the opposite direction, downriver, the Musée des Égouts (Sewer Museum) in Anderlecht gives access to the vaulted tunnel enclosing the river. A little further on, La Grande Écluse restaurant gives some idea of the former lock that regulated the level of the Senne's waters within Brussels. This was in fact the first vaulted section of the river. And still further downriver, at the house at 23 rue Saint-Géry you can see one of the river's disused channels.

NEARBY

Anderlecht Municipal Hall ⑧

Place du Conseil 1
02 558 08 00

All too often, business with the various administrative services at the Anderlect Municipal Hall makes you forget the architectural and patrimonial treasures on display there. To have a look around (free), usually you only need to ask politely. The other solutions are to ask if you can attend the meetings of the local council itself (they are open to the public), or more drastically, get married there, as the council chamber also serves as the registry office.

Inaugurated by King Léopold II in 1879 in the presence of bourgmestre Van Lint, the Municipal Hall was built in the neo-Renaissance style by the architect Van Ysendijck and has a 48 m belfry. The remarkable council chamber with its beautiful stained-glass windows and sculptures by Constantin Meunier is reason enough for a visit.

NATIONAL MUSEUM OF THE RESISTANCE

Sorrow and pity

Rue Van Lint 14
02 522 40 41
Monday to Friday 9am–12pm and 1pm–4pm, Wednesday by reservation
Metro Clémenceau

Under-publicized, old-fashioned and poorly presented as it may be, the National Museum of the Resistance is nevertheless a place from which you emerge in a state of shock. While the museum provides a general overview of the Resistance movement in Belgium during the Second World War, it is the force, and even violence, of its photos that remains its most remarkable feature. The series portraying the prisoners of concentration camps comes close to the unbearable, including one showing a German doctor performing an experiment on a prisoner by injecting substances directly into the skull with a syringe. Others reveal the state of the gas chambers, taken upon the arrival of Allied forces, filled by heaps of mangled, wasted bodies.

The museum also offers a very realistic account of the Resistance movement itself, with details of certain sabotage operations, identity cards used by Resistance members, etc. You'll probably find yourselves the only visitors in the museum. Take advantage of this by asking the curator, Monsieur Bouchez, to tell you more about the various items on display. And take time to reflect on a desperate moment in human history. We mention in passing that the museum premises used to be printing works.

BUILDINGS OF THE FORMER ATLAS BREWERY

A social concoction

Rue du Libre Examen 15 – 02 523 80 45 – lapoudriere.org
Donations Monday, Tuesday and Friday 2pm–6pm
Metro Aumale

Not far from the canal and place de la Vaillance, the pretty buildings of the former Atlas brewery are today occupied by the members of the Emmaüs charitable organization. So you can not only visit this industrial heritage site, but you can also leave items that you no longer require. The principle on which Emmaüs works is familiar: helping people in need by selling various second-hand household goods at unbeatable prices. Launched in 1912 by the Saint-Guidon brewery, the construction of the buildings here was not completed until 1926. Although the brewing and fermentation rooms along with the conservation chambers had been built, the stables, offices and rinsing rooms were only finished in 1924. Last of all, in 1926, a 30 m tower in Art Deco style was added, marking the transition to a new technique for brewing beer. Meanwhile, the Saint-Guidon brewery became the Atlas brewery, which continued at this site until 1952. The operation was then taken over by the Haecht brewing company and the buildings were used for warehousing bottles and crates. And in 1980 all activities here ceased and the buildings are now used as a warehouse by the Communauté de la Poudrière, a 'self-managed community seeking to experiment with an alternative to capitalism and individualism, where human beings are once again the priority'.

JUSTICE DE PAIX

Beneath the fine vaulting of Justice, all hearings are public

Place de la Résistance 3
Entry possible during public hearings: Tuesday and Thursday mornings, as well as every other Monday and Wednesday, starting at 9am
Metro Saint-Guidon

Constructed in 1893 to plans by the architect E. S'Jonghers, the Justice de Paix building is characterized by its neo-Renaissance style. Although a familiar sight to the residents of Anderlecht, few are aware that you can visit the courtrooms or watch cases being pleaded.

Having gained considerable economic importance by the end of the 20th century, Anderlecht was designated as the centre for administrating justice in the canton (now divided into two) in 1890. Since then, all the minor legal conflicts arising in Anderlecht have been judged here. The coats of arms of all these communes are represented on the façade, just beneath the first-floor lintels.

© Jacquesverlaeken

Cases from the first canton are heard on Thursday mornings and those from the second canton on Tuesday mornings, in the chambers on the first floor. The cases heard on these two days involve simple civil matters such as disputes over rents, alimony, insurance premiums and bills. It's an excellent opportunity to admire this very handsome room with an *entrevous* (decorated plaster) ceiling supported by steel beams. Those who'd like to see how the Belgian judicial system actually works might be better off attending hearings of more complex and interesting cases. These take place every other Wednesday at 9am for the first canton, and at the same time every other Monday for the second canton.

All these hearings are open to the public.

NEARBY
Houses at rue du Greffe 26–32 ⑫

Built in 1899–1900 by Anderlecht architect E. Fouarge, and his only major achievement, these four houses form a handsome set of single-family workers' homes in the Art Nouveau style. The terracotta medallions at No. 26, representing an owl taking flight and a rooster, are particularly memorable. The floral motifs at No. 28, along with its balconies, also deserve a closer look. At the corner of rue du Greffe and rue du Village, you'll also come across a pretty bas-relief representing the crow and the fox from La Fontaine's fable.

SAINT GUY, CRYPT AND TOMB

*Slip beneath the saint's cenotaph to have
your prayers answered*

Collégiale Saints-Pierre-et-Guidon d'Anderlecht
Place de la Vaillance
The church is open daily, 9.30am–12pm and 2pm–4.30pm (closed Wednesday)
To visit the crypt, find the sexton who has the keys
Metro Saint Guidon

The famous Gothic collegial church dedicated to St Peter and St Guy, which stands on Place de la Vaillance, has long been the nerve centre of the village of Anderlecht and a fruitful pilgrimage site. Although its façade is quite familiar to residents, few know that the edifice hides an unusual crypt that is open to visitors. A stairway to the right of the main altar thus takes you back to the Roman period of the late 6th century.

This rather large crypt crowned by semi-circular vaults is dimly lit by the light that filters through its small windows, a fact that some believe proves that this wasn't originally a crypt, but an older church that was later covered by the current Gothic edifice. Note that some of the columns are monoliths, made of a single piece of stone; they probably came from an even older structure and were reused here. They surround a strange, empty tomb that, tradition says, was that of St Guy himself.

It is composed of a trapezoid slab with supports creating a narrow passage that pilgrims took in order to ask the saint to answer their prayers (note how the stones are worn down at this spot). If you have prayers that need answering, don't hesitate to slip through this narrow passage as well.

Saint Guy

This man, who would one day become the patron saint of the village of Anderlecht, was born in Anderlecht sometime around AD 950 to a poor rural family. He became famous for his miracles as well as for his pilgrimage to the Holy Land.

When he died on 12 September 1012, the Anderlecht church was just a modest chapel. Over time, news of the miracles attributed to the saint spread and an increasingly large number of pilgrims came to beseech his aid to cure dysentery (of which he had died on his return from Jerusalem), contagious diseases and the diseases that decimated the livestock and horses. There were so many visitors that the parish prospered and was able to build a collegial church worthy of the largest dioceses. Inside the church there are several depictions of the saint and his life in the stained-glass windows, frescoes and sculptures.

CHINA MUSEUM

Missionaries in China sent objects home to educate their colleagues

Chaussée de Ninove 548
02 526 14 00
Open by arrangement
Admission free
Bus F, Scheut stop; M or R bus, Obus stop

L ocated in the modern and rather charmless building that houses the Ordre des Missionnaires de Scheut, the China Museum nevertheless warrants a visit due to the very high quality of its collections.

This museum owes its existence to the missionary order of Scheut, whose objective was to spread the Christian Gospel throughout China. Founded in 1862 by Père Théophile Verbist as the Congrégation Missionnaire du Cœur-Immaculé-de-Marie, the Ordre de Scheut, as it is known today, is named after 'Scheutveld', the Anderlecht neighbourhood where the order's first house was built.

Before being sent to China, the missionaries received an introduction to the Chinese language and culture according to the precepts of Père Verbist, for whom linguistic knowledge, respect for identity and cultural adaptation were fundamental. For this reason, he insisted that each missionary in the field in China send objects back to Belgium, to help in the training of future recruits. This practice was the origin of the museum.

Divided into four sections ('language and writing', 'daily life', 'local religious beliefs', and 'spreading the Gospels'), the museum presents objects of rare quality. There is notably an extraordinary collection of Chinese artefacts, some of which date back to 2500 BC. Then there is the showcase that describes the famous practice of foot binding inflicted on Chinese women, forced to respect a rather peculiar canon of beauty, along with various examples of footwear that accompanied this custom. Opposite, the technical virtuosity of an unusual ivory ball leaves you dumbfounded. The superb porcelains and statues, including a beautiful bronze Buddha cast in 1457, are also admirable.

And don't miss the room right next to the museum, which contains portraits of over 3,000 missionaries who have carried out the work of the Ordre de Scheut.

Impressive.

CITÉ-JARDIN DE MOORTEBEEK

A country air

Boulevard Shakespeare and surrounding streets
Bus 46

Built in an outlying Anderlecht district in 1922, the Cité-Jardin de Moortebeek is today a pleasant neighbourhood, despite a relative lack of shops. A succession of homes each with its own garden, their characteristic yolk colour makes it easy to pick out the boundaries of the settlement. Following a competition won by Jean-François Hoeben, the design of the garden city was shared among seven different architects in order to prevent too much monotony from creeping in: Hoeben was responsible for rue de l'Agronome, the beginning of rue Sévigné, the lower part of rue Horace and the eastern section of avenue Shakespeare; Bragard for rue Horace; Mouton for rue Virgile and the middle section of avenue Shakespeare; Verlant and De Paepe for rue Homère, rue de Lamartine, and the part of rue de Sévigné close to La Tourelle; Diongre for rue Corneille and the western section of avenue Shakespeare; and lastly Brunfaut for rues Ronsard, Rabelais and Tolstoï, as well as the south side of boulevard Shakespeare.

Built to the same specifications, these 330 houses and 124 flats all have similar layouts: a basement with two cellars, a ground floor with a common living room with an area of at least 16 m², a laundry room, a kitchen, a WC and a hall. Although the houses had no bathroom, the laundry room had to include a shower. The kitchens themselves were not very large. The Cité-Jardin de Moortebeek had been incorporated into the rest of the city by the 1970s.

NEARBY
Cité Bon Air

Located behind Le Ring and along avenue d'Itterbeek, around place Séverine
Bus No. 46, Sibelius stop

Designed by the architect Voets, the Cité Bon Air was built in several stages. The first and most important took place in 1923 with the construction of a group of 208 houses. More accommodation was added in 1930 (122 houses), 1938 (36), in the period 1945–50 (40) and in 1953 (33). It was originally intended to rehouse residents whose homes were demolished to make way for the Nord-Midi rail link in the centre of Brussels.

© Ben2

Cités-jardins

The Garden City Movement was born in England at the end of the 19th century, largely inspired by the ideas of Ebenezer Howard. In Belgium, the first garden city was Winterslag, built by Adrien Blomme in 1912. But it was actually between 1918 and 1930 that the movement took off in Belgium, particularly in the Brussels region. In the aftermath of the devastation caused by the First World War and faced with a housing deficit of 200,000 homes, priority was given to garden cities. The employment minister Joseph Wauters declared in 1920: 'The ideal we seek is to provide everyone with a dwelling, a home in a particularly attractive environment, surrounded by trees, light, and greenery.' The garden cities were thus not only a solution to the lack of workers' housing, but were also seen as a means of transforming the structure of society by offering them an environment that would favour their emancipation. Led by the town planner and landscaper Louis Van der Swaelmen and architects including Eggerickx, Hoste, De

Ligne, Hoeben, Rubbers and Pompe, a ring of 25 garden cities as well as other housing projects inspired by this movement were built in the Brussels suburbs. Many of these projects were launched at the initiative of tenants' cooperatives, including both these famous garden cities in Watermael-Boitsfort. Others were created by the local communes as social housing schemes. If simplicity and economy were the guiding principles in the construction of these garden cities, they were also an opportunity for some interesting technical experiments: working to a limited budget, architects were forced to stretch their imagination to optimize the internal layout and facilities of the dwellings, and to find a compromise between individual housing units and community space. Although today some garden cities in the Brussels region have become desirable residences, it must not be forgotten that when they first saw the light of day these neighbourhoods were a long way from the city centre and transport links were poor. It was only in the 1970s that they became fully integrated into the spreading urban network.

© Lampa 21

LOURDES GROTTO

Bernadette and Marie at the edge of the ring road

Rue de la Floraison
Bus No. 46, Pommier stop

Rue de la Floraison, which is bordered by an elegant alley of linden trees, was an integral part of a late 19th-century project to create a series of ring roads in Brussels that was never carried out. Today, the road is a dead end that offers a view of the ring road that was eventually built in 1978 about a hundred metres below.

In 1914, a church dedicated to Saint Gerard Majella was built here to serve the Neerpede district, which had no parish of its own. The church was renovated into its current state in 1952 and has since been a Dutch-speaking parish. In 1916, a school was also built and was run by the nuns who lived in the adjoining building.

The 'Lourdes grotto', located just in front of these buildings in a small clearing, probably dates from this period. This artificial grotto with its little benches is an imitation of the original one at Lourdes and commemorates the apparition of the Holy Virgin to Bernadette Soubirous in 1858. Its workmanship is delightfully clumsy, as you can see the brick structure beneath the thick concrete. As its cared-for condition and lit candles indicate, the grotto is still a site of worship today.

Anderlecht beyond the ring road

Anderlecht is the only Brussels village to cross the west ring road towards the hills of Pajottenland. This zone of over 400 hectares bordering Leeuw-Saint-Pierre and Dilbeek is still semi-rural. It is an immense open-air museum that reveals what the western and northern areas of the Brussels region looked like before the city became industrialized and urbanized. Here, the urban landscape gives way to the hilly countryside of the Pajottenland, which is criss-crossed by two valleys, the Vogelenzangbeek to the south and the Pede to the north, around which lies the village of Neerpede. With just a few exceptions, the landscape is the same as the one that enchanted Breughel in the 16th century. Curiously, you can even get here by taking the metro (line 1B, Erasme stop). Be sure to bring sturdy footwear or a bike.

MAURICE CARÊME MUSEUM

Passion and poetry

Avenue Nellie Melba 14b
mauricecareme.be
Only by booking at 02 521 67 75 (Madame Jeannine Burny)
Admission free
Metro Veeweyde

Born in 1899 to a house painter and a grocer, Maurice Carême was by no means predestined for writing. He was a brilliant pupil and, by age 15, was already composing his first verses. It was an activity he pursued for the rest of his life.

Today, Carême is internationally renowned for his writing aimed at young people and his texts expressing the greatness and misery of mankind.

In 1972, he was elected 'Prince of Poets' at the Café Procope in Paris, as evidenced by a commemorative plaque on the façade of the famous cafe.

Carême died in 1978 and, in addition to his wonderful writings, he left behind a house-museum that is a delight to visit, as it has remained as it was when he lived there.

Shortly before his death, Carême and his closest friends set up a foundation to promote his writings and preserve his archives. He also wanted his house to remain an open place to live, particularly for the children he hoped would be inspired to take up poetry.

The 'White House', as it is known today, was built in the image of the old houses in the poet's native Brabant. It contains period furniture, knick-knacks and old crockery, as well as numerous portraits of the poet, most of them painted by great Belgian artists he counted among his friends. These include works by De Boeck, Delvaux and Wolvens. In addition to the poet's living environment, the museum also features an archive room, a library specialising in poetry from around the world, sound and audio-visual documents and manuscripts.

LE 4 MAI 1999

LE BANQUET DES POÈTES
CÉLÈBRE AU PROCOPE
LE CENTENAIRE DE LA NAISSANCE
DE MAURICE CARÊME
PRINCE EN POÉSIE
1899 ~ 1999

The art of gardening

Avenue Marius Renard 1
02 526 75 00
Usually open from the second weekend in May
Metro Veeweyde – Tram No. 56, Debussy stop

Only two minutes from Anderlecht stadium, the Institut Redouté is a little-known school of horticulture, and a very pleasant place for a walk. Although in theory visits are only possible on those days when the school opens its doors to the public, you can sometimes get in by asking nicely.

Don't be put off by the unappealing façade visible from the street. The heart of matters at this school lie behind the building, spread out over 4 hectares of grounds. You can walk to the left via the greenhouses or to the right through superb vegetable plots. An additional attraction of this place is that you will probably find yourself on your own and thus free to quietly stroll along the pretty lanes, among flowers, bushes and fragrant plants.

Be sure to admire in particular the famous rocaille (rockery), of which the Institut is justly proud. Created in the 1960s by the architect de Witte, it boasts a series of rocks, lawns, cedars, rhododendrons, larches and gingkos.

The Institut dates back to 1913, the idea being to provide training for the children of market gardeners, but the first classes were not organized until 1922, in a building in Parc Astrid called *La Laiterie* (The Dairy). Students applied their knowledge on 2 hectares of ground located on avenue de Neerpede. Since 1995, the Institut has come under the wing of the Commission Communautaire Française (governing body for the French-speaking community in Belgium).

Pierre-Joseph Redouté

Born in 1759, Redouté was one of the most renowned 19th-century painters of flowers. In 1804, he was named official flower painter for the French Empress, Napoleon's wife Josephine, who commissioned him in 1813 to paint the ephemeral beauty of the famous roses of Malmaison, her favourite residence. This would remain his best-known work. A member of the Légion d'Honneur and later knighted by the Belgian Ordre de Léopold, he died in 1840.

CITÉ-JARDIN DE LA ROUE

Freewheeling

Various streets near place Ministre Wauters
Metro La Roue

With its Art Deco houses, along with its lanes, paths and green spaces, the Cité-Jardin de la Roue bears glowing testimony to progressive town planning at the beginning of the 20th century. Constructed from 1920 onwards to plans drafted by the architects Pompe, Meckmans, Jonghers and Voets for an 18 hectare site, this garden city owes its name to an inn called *La Roue* (The Wheel) which in the 18th centry stood at the crossing of chaussée de Mons and chaussée de Lennick, opposite a windmill.

The garden city corresponded to a certain ideal of emancipation for the working class at the time, based on the theories of the town planner Louis Van der Swaelmen. Each organized along the same lines (shared living room, three bedrooms, and 50 m² garden), the 688 single-family homes in the garden city constituted a homogeneous group with street names that evoked the concerns and goals of the class struggle at the time: rues des Droits de l'Homme, de la Solidarité, des Plébéiens, etc.

Start your working tour at 101 rue des Colombophiles, where pleasant vegetable gardens allow a clear view towards the canal. The area just to the south has numerous lanes, sometimes rather poorly maintained but charming just the same. There are access points to them on the left at 50 rue des Citoyens, to the left again at 43 avenue des Plébéiens, and from avenue des Colombophiles, almost at the corner with avenue des Plébéiens, just before the railway bridge.

After this railway bridge, there's a little path that starts just to the left of 10 rue de la Tranquillité. This street name is quite apt, and any barking dogs should probably avoid this part of the tour. At the end of the path, you'll emerge at 28 rue des Grives, just in front of the CERIA buildings. Lastly, not too far away, at 21 rue de la Solidarité, another lane takes you as far as 19 rue Hoorickx. And there are more lanes to be found, notably around the plaine des Loisirs.

NEARBY

La Roue School (21)

Rue Van Winghen 1

Built in 1938 according to plans drafted by the architect Henri Wildenblanck, the La Roue School (École de la Roue), which forms part of the La Roue Garden Suburb, is a fine example of a school built in the Art Deco style. The playground, which may usually be visited on request, has a splendid stained glass window by F. Crickx showing children playing. Also note the remarkable arch dating from 1960 to the right of the entrance door: it bears an eloquent explanation that education is compulsory.

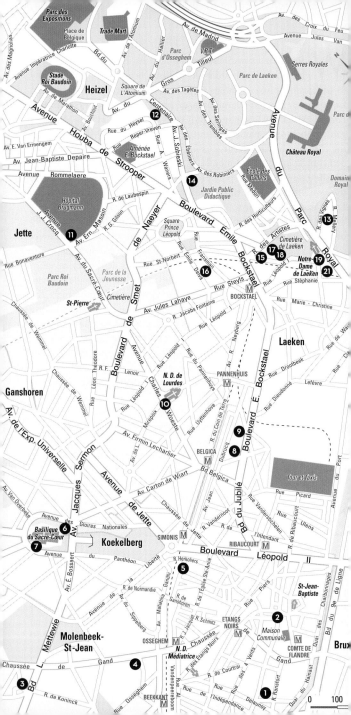

Molenbeek, Koekelberg, Laeken

BRUSSELS MUSEUM
OF INDUSTRY AND LABOUR

Molenbeek, land of working-class immigration

Rue de Ransfort 27
02 410 99 50 – lafonderie.be
During exhibitions the museum is open Tuesday to Friday 10am–5pm,
Saturday and Sunday 2pm–5pm, closed Monday
Exterior of site accessible Monday to Friday 9am–5pm
Admission: free, except during exhibitions
Metro Comte de Flandre – Tram No. 81, 82 – Bus No. 88, 89

The Brussels Museum of Industry and Labour owes its existence to the dynamic heritage association, La Fonderie, which took over these premises of the former Compagnie des Bronzes in 1983. Don't turn away if you get the impression that the museum is closed. Push open the gate and you'll find the reception area to the right, at the back of the yard.

Apart from the turners' hall, the museum has today become a sort of garden full of a certain 'romantic' industrial charm. Some handsome buildings in ruins give a sense of the activities that once took place here. A statue of Roosevelt cast at this very site can be seen through some broken windows, defying the passage of time. Various machines are still lying around in the overgrown grass, forming an unkempt little industrial cemetery.

The current exhibition (the theme changes every year) relates the history of Molenbeek, recalling in particular the condition of the working classes in the past. The presence of the curator with his shrewd commentary greatly enhances the tour.

Once the Charleroi canal was dug in 1832, Molenbeek, nicknamed the 'Little Manchester' of Belgium in 1890, began to take in large numbers of immigrants from both the Flanders and Wallonia regions of Belgium, but also from France, Italy, and Spain.

La Compagnie des Bronzes was established here in 1854. Specializing in the production of art objects and furnishings in bronze, zinc and other metals, it also made components for lighting and heating by gas or electricity. From 1870, the company expanded its business to include casting monumental statues. Among other artists, Jef Lambeaux and Constantin Meunier made use of its services. The doors of the Palais de Justice, the lions of the Colonne du Congrès, the equestrian statue of King Albert I at Le Mont des Arts and of Leopold II at place du Trône, as well as the statues of Le Petit Sablon, are just some of the famous Brussels pieces that were cast here. And overseas, the company also made the 28 ton gates for the New York Zoo.

After the First World War, orders declined sharply and the company finally closed down in 1979.

②

NEARBY

Former shop Aux 100 000 Chemises

Rue Comte de Flandre 38

Even if you're feeling perfectly fit, don't hesitate to visit this establishment, now a health centre: the beautiful frontage of this former shirt shop conceals handsome furnishings that have been partly preserved.

CITÉ DIONGRE / CITÉ SAULNIER ③

Picturesque cottage-style housing

Rue Joseph Diongre
Place Leroy – Rue de Bruges
Metro Beekkant

Cité Diongre, at the junction of boulevard Mettewie and chaussée de Gand, was built by the official architect for the commune of Molenbeek, Joseph Diongre, in 1922. Diongre (1878–1963) is known primarily for designing the Institut National de Radiodiffusion at place Flagey in Ixelles and the Saint-Jean-Baptiste church in Molenbeek. The Cité was built in response to a commission from the commune which at the time was attempting to cope with the damage caused by the First World War. To this end, Diongre created a picturesque social housing estate with both flats and detached houses, in a very harmonious cottage style. Note the naive bas-reliefs next to the doors, which commemorate a port, an activity, or a planet of the solar system. These dwellings are set among greenery that provides a sharp contrast with the huge buildings nearby. The Cité Diongre, however, can no longer be considered a true garden city: in 1930, a violent storm blew down a large number of trees surrounding the estate. Adjoining the Cité Diongre, the Cité de Saulnier also resembles a garden city but in a slightly different style. Bordered by rues De Saulnier, Potaerdegat, Béguine and Korenbeek, the buildings have a greyer, more uniform appearance less appealing than the neighbouring estate. Note the large porch leading to the interior of one of the housing blocks.

NEARBY

Rue Jules Delhaize (4)

A handsome group of workers' homes built by the architect Vereecke. They offer some pretty sgraffiti, but unfortunately most of them have been clumsily restored. Constructed in 1904 to house the workers at the Coster et Clément shirt factory, which lies right in the middle of this city block, these homes look almost as if they belong at the seaside. Their architect was inspired by the style of houses he had already built at Middelkerke on the Belgian coast. The shirt factory closed down completely in 1946, while the Générale de Banque began installing its printing services there from 1940.

THE FORMER KOEKELBERG MUNICIPAL GIRLS' SCHOOL

Exceptional yet largely unknown sgraffiti

Rue Herkoliers 35 et 37
Koekelberg

Listed in 2008, the former Koekelberg municipal girls' school was built in the Art Nouveau style by Henri Jacobs at the same time as the municipal school on rue Josaphat in Schaerbeek in 1907.

The old school was made up of two buildings: the school entrance and the caretaker's accommodation were at No. 35, and the headmistress' accommodation could be found at No. 37. The façade of No. 35 features a magnificent sgraffito depicting an owl (symbol of knowledge) with outstretched wings above a five-pointed star (a pentagram, symbol

© EmDee

of spiritual fulfilment, which in this case is linked to self-knowledge), surrounded by stylised floral and plant motifs. At No. 37, under the dormer window, is another owl, this time with its eyes closed and its wings folded. In contrast to the owl on the other façade, this perhaps signifies that self-knowledge, which leads to spiritual fulfilment, involves first observing oneself (with eyes closed, turned inwards) and one's immediate surroundings (hence the folded wings) before being able to really take flight?

Today, the school is home to a number of organisations, and it is usually possible to access the former courtyard to admire the spectacular sgraffito frieze running around the perimeter, the work of Adolphe Crespin (1909). Most of the world is represented through animals from almost every continent: Oceania (kangaroos, lyrebirds, buffalo and ostriches), America (bison, marmots, mustangs, sheep and condor), Europe (bears, wolves, deer, hare, bees), Asia (tiger, cobra, crocodile, rhinoceros, flamingo, peacock) and Africa (elephants, ostriches, lions,

monkeys, parrots).

To the right of the sgraffito representing Asia is a swastika encircled by a snake biting its tail (ouroboros). The swastika, before being hijacked by the Nazis, was a symbol that originated in Asia thousands of years ago. As for the ouroboros, it is a fascinating, little-known symbol that relates to the theme of the eternal return and spiritual enlightenment.

For more information on the swastika and the ouroboros, see opposite and on next double page.

© EmDee

The swastika: a symbol of life and regeneration

The word swastika comes from Sanskrit and means 'auspicious' (according to the Larousse dictionary) or 'conducive to well-being' (according to the Encyclopedia Universalis). The symbol is among the most widespread and oldest symbols in the world. It can be found on Mesopotamian coins and in Christian and Byzantine art, where it is known as the 'cross gammadion', because its branches recall the Greek letter 'gamma'. Without claiming to be exhaustive, this symbol can also be found among the Celts, the Etruscans, Northern Europe, Central America (the Mayans) and North America (the Navajo Indians), China and India. Finally, some believe that the true (natural) origin of the symbol lies in Tibet: the cross was simply 'drawn' on the slopes of the mythical Mount Kailas in Western Tibet, a sacred mountain for Hindus and Buddhists who regard it as the centre of the world. Usually, the symbolism of this design relates to the idea of rotation around a fixed point, the centre of the cross. In this sense, some people suggest it evokes the Self, the Center, the Wheel or the Sun, while also insisting on its dynamic nature, which suggests rotation, movement and, beyond that, action, regeneration and the cycles of life and nature. The other major characteristic of this symbol lies in its dual nature, depending on the orientation of its branches. When the arms of the cross are oriented to the left, meaning with a rotation from left to right (clockwise) or from East to West, the icon is called a swastika. But when the arms are oriented in the other direction (counterclockwise), the icon is called a *sauvastika*. In the first case, the swastika accompanies beneficial deities and 'positive' phenomena such as the day or creation while the version that rotates counterclockwise represents the night, the goddess Kali in the Hindu religion, and generally has darker connotations.

The choice of the swastika as a Nazi emblem

The Nazi party theorist Alfred Rosenberg (1893-1946) was instrumental in the choice of the swastika as the Nazi symbol as he attributed Germanic descent to the Aryans (a linguistic group that lived in Central Asia around the 3rd millennium BC). For the Orientalist Émile Burnouf, the swastika was the symbol of the Aryans, whom he described as a superior 'race' with pantheistic tendencies, as opposed to the 'race' of monotheistic Semites. Hitler saw it as the 'symbol of the struggle for the victory of the Aryan'.

The Ouroboros: a symbol of divine illumination

The figure of a coiled serpent biting its own tail is sometimes found in iconography and literature. This symbol is traditionally known as the *Ouroboros* or *Uroboros*, a Greek word derived from the Coptic and Hebrew languages – *ouro* is Coptic for 'king' and *ob* Hebrew for 'serpent' – meaning 'royal serpent'. Thus the reptile raising its head above its body is used as a symbol of mystical illumination: for Eastern peoples, it represents the divine fire they call Kundalini. Kundalini is the origin of the association that Western medicine of the Middle Ages and Renaissance made between, on the one hand, the body heat that rises from the base of the spine to the top of the head and, on the other, the *venena bibas* ('ingested venom' mentioned by Saint Benedict of Nursia) of the snake whose bite can only be treated by an equally potent poison. Just as the Eastern techniques of spiritual awakening, Dzogchen and Mahamudra, show how a meditating person must learn to 'bite his tail like the serpent', the theme of the *Ouroboros* and ingested venom is a reminder that spiritual awareness can only result from a devout life: by elevating your consciousness onto a mental plane surpassing the ordinary, you search within to truly find yourself as an eternal being. The Greeks popularised the word ouroboros in its literal sense of 'serpent biting its tail'. They acquired this image from the Phoenicians through contact with the Hebrews, who had themselves adopted it from Egypt where the *Ouroboros* featured on a stele dated as early as 1600 BC. There it represented the sun god Ra (Light), who resurrects life from the darkness of the night (synonymous with death), going back to the theme of eternal return, life, death, and the renewal of existence, as well as the reincarnation of souls in successive human bodies until they have reached their evolutionary peak, which will leave them perfect, both physically and spiritually – a theme dear to Eastern peoples.

In this sense, the serpent swallowing itself can also be interpreted as an interruption of the cycle of human development (represented by the serpent) in order to enter the cycle of spiritual evolution (represented by the circle).

Pythagoras associated the serpent with the mathematical concept of infinity, coiled up as zero – the abstract number used to denote eternity, which becomes reality when the *Ouroboros* is depicted turning around on itself.

Gnostic Christians identified it with the Holy Spirit revealed through wisdom to be the Creator of all things visible and invisible, and whose ultimate expression on Earth is Christ. For this reason, the symbol is associated in Greek Gnostic literature with the phrase *hen to pan* (The All is One); it was commonly adopted in the 4th and 5th centuries as a protective amulet against evil spirits and venomous snakebites. This amulet was known as Abraxas, the name of a god in the original Gnostic pantheon that the Egyptians recognise as Serapis. It became one of the most famous magical talismans of the Middle Ages.

Greek alchemists very quickly espoused the figure of the *Ouroboros* and so it reached the Hermetic philosophers of Alexandria – among them, Arab thinkers who studied and disseminated this image in their schools of Hermeticism and alchemy.

These schools were known and sought out by medieval Christians. There is even historical evidence that members of the Order of the Knights Templar, as well as other Christian mystics, travelled to Cairo, Syria and even Jerusalem to be initiated into the Hermetic sciences.

BASEMENTS OF THE SACRED HEART BASILICA

Potholing at the Koekelberg basilica

Parvis de la Basilique 1
Daily 8am–6pm (5pm in winter)
ASBL Groupe Spéléo Redan : 02 414 45 59
gs-redan.net
Potholing sessions every first and third Monday of the month
Hire of rooms: 02 425 88 22
Library open Sunday 9.45am–11.30am and 4pm–5pm
Parish cloakroom open Thursday 2pm–3.30pm
Mass celebrated daily at 9am in the small chapel (door 1)
Metro Simonis ou tram No. 19

The basements of the Koekelberg basilica, the fifth-largest church in the world (after Saint Peter's in Rome, Notre-Dame- de-la-Paix

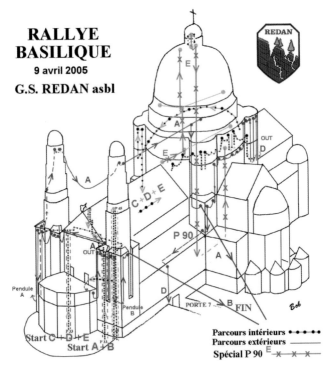

- 234 -

in Yamoussoukro (Ivory Coast), Saint Paul's in London, and Santa-Maria in Florence) conceal a completely undreamed-of world: a theatre, meeting rooms, a bar, scouts' quarters, offices, a laundry, a library, a cloakroom, the diaconal secretariat (you can reserve Masses there), a bridge club, and a free Catholic radio station, but in particular a really surreal potholing club!

The association, the Groupe Spéléo Redan, is to be found in a room originally used to stock coal for heating, behind a heavy metal door (entry – door 7). Behind this door, you'll come across a surprising scene: these potholers don't hesitate to use old drainpipes, narrow service stairs, and even a chimney measuring barely a metre in diameter, to climb 30 metres higher, like mice in Swiss cheese. The association meets here on the first and third Monday of each month, and every three years they hold a big rally: the entire basilica (both inside and out) is then taken over by potholers.

Other than these events, members volunteer their assistance and skills during renovation work, when this involves reaching particularly inaccessible spots.

Normally, however, the best way to visit the basements is to attend the Mass that takes place in the little underground chapel, door 1.

NEARBY

Sœurs Noires Museum ⑦

In summer, Wednesday 2pm–4pm
Or by arrangement to 02 425 88 22

On the first floor of the Koekelberg basilica, this tiny museum, the size of a small room, contains a collection of dishes, cooking utensils, porcelain, relics, lace, jewels, sceptres, paintings and furniture from the cloister of the Sœurs Noires in Brussels. During the French Revolution, these nuns were allowed to preserve their treasures in recognition of their aid to plague victims. Dating back to the 14th century, the convent was closed in 1998 due to the dwindling number of sisters living there and it was converted into an old people's home. A timeless place to visit.

FINE FAÇADES IN
AVENUE JEAN DUBRUCQ

Little-known mosaics and ceramics

Avenue Jean Dubrucq 23, 75 and 206
Boulevard du Jubilé 157
Metro Belgica or Pannenhuis

Avenue Jean Dubrucq, away from the traditional tourist sights, runs through what is today a deprived neighbourhood on the border between Molenbeek and Jette. It nevertheless displays some little known yet handsome façades. The house at No. 23 has superb ceramic tiles representing a female archer in a forest, with birds. A little further on, at No. 75, Villa Cléo has some pretty Art Nouveau ceramics portraying a woman's head. Eastwards, the street becomes more industrial and less attractive in character. But at No. 206 an Art Deco building can be found with some astonishing mosaics depicting a spider in its web and butterflies. Continuing down the street a little way towards Laeken, note the surprising sailboat used as a shop sign, just before the bridge. This bridge offers an unusual view of the centre of Brussels. In the foreground, vegetable gardens stand out in front of the 'Tour et Taxis' site and against the business district around the Gare du Nord. Not far from there, at 57 boulevard du Jubilé, some beautiful mosaics represent two peacocks displaying.

© EmDee

NEARBY
Former Besse warehouse
⑨

Rue de l'Escaut 122

The former wine warehouse for the *Société Besse Père et Fils*, this attractive industrial building was constructed in 1908 by the architect J. Rau. Converted by Jo Crépin in 1997, it's occupied today by the VVL BBDO advertising agency. Sometimes it's possible to go inside and admire the handsome space created by this successful renovation. A good excuse might be to say that you're seeking information about the original company.

WITHUIS

An architectural oddity

Avenue Charles Woeste 183
Jette

Opposite the Notre-Dame-de-Lourdes church in Jette, the Withu (White House) is a surprisingly modernist building which wa designed in 1927 by the architect Joseph Diongre (1878–1963). Listed i 1985 (the exterior and the interior are listed, which means the furnitu cannot leave the premises), the house was designed for the writer J

ennekens (1877–1943) and his family, who were friends of Diongre. Iennekens was a Flemish-speaking poet and the municipal secretary r Molenbeek-Saint-Jean.

The strikingly original façade combines modernist influences (with the it roof and entablature windows so typical of Le Corbusier's doctrine, as oked in his architecture manifesto 'Five Points of Architecture'), cubism he very pronounced volumes), Art Deco and Streamline Moderne.

There are also some interesting details, such as the ironwork (by F. arion) framing the entrance staircase, which incorporates the street umber on either side, and an inkwell with a quill dipped in it, in ference to the poet's work.

The front door is decorated with geometric motifs and the poet's ionogram, while the left-hand side bears the name of the house, Vithuis', in highly stylised letters.

The interior, which cannot be sited, is unique because it too was esigned by the architect. In fact,)iongre was responsible for the esign of the interior decoration, the irniture, the stained-glass windows by Jettois glassmaker Fernand Crickx, ased on drawings by Diongre), the ght fittings and the ceramics, making he house a complete work of art.

Joseph Diongre

After the war, Diongre played a part in the social housing construction movement and was involved in the construction of many buildings in Laeken (1920 and 1923), Saint-Gilles (1922), Anderlecht (1922), Molenbeek (1924 and 1927) and the garden city that bears his name in Molenbeek (1922).

From 1925 on, Diongre designed some of the most characteristic buildings of the inter-war period in Brussels in a tempered, modernist style: the Withuis in Jette (1927), the Saint-Jean-Baptiste church in Molenbeek (1930) and the famous National Radio Broadcasting Institute (INR) in Ixelles (1933–1938).

The name 'Withuis' refers to the 'Zwart Huis' (Black House) constructed in Knokke by the architect Huib Hoste, a contemporary of Diongre.

QUEEN ELISABETH MEDICAL FOUNDATION

Take a look and you'll start feeling better!

Avenue J.J. Crocq 1–3
fmre-gske.be
Open weekdays during office hours
Bus No. 53 or 88, Crocq stop

The Queen Elisabeth Medical Foundation, originally a site f
scientific research, is part of the Brugmann Hospital compl
designed by Victor Horta beginning in 1912. The complex has since bee
greatly transformed by modern buildings. With its numerous laboratorie
the foundation was meant to strengthen the links between the researche
and the doctors of this vast hospital. Many residents still know little abo
this highly original building designed in 1926 by Henri Lacoste, one
Belgium's leading Art Deco architects. The architecture of this publ
building gives a new, unique meaning to the term the 'Roaring Twentie
Indeed, few artists were able to bring their dreams to life so poeticall
especially for a hospital laboratory.

The long, brick-red façades with their colourful tapered ceramic ghlights exude imagination. Yet they offer only a hint of the magic dden inside, where Lacoste exploited all the possible uses of a newly veloped material – marbrite. This coloured, opaque glass, the result of technique developed in Hainaut, was all the rage in the interwar period at its popularity quickly fell. As its name indicates, this material was eant to imitate marble in infinitely richer tones at a markedly cheaper rice. Lacoste streaked the luminous columns and walls with contrasting ripes of blue, green and white, the design of which cleverly blends to that of the stained-glass windows. On the first floor, the entrance the library goes a step further with its pink and black marbrite. It lays with more traditional proportions, however. The red terrazzo* anister, with its heavy forms, solidifies the general composition of the bby. In complete contrast to the hospital's clean rooms covered in cold aterials, the first floor library offers a cosy atmosphere.

Although the lobby and nearby areas are generally accessible during ie week, you should politely ask for permission to take a look.

Also typical of the interwar period, terrazzo is made by adding crushed marble of various colours to concrete.

SYLVAN THEATRE
AND OSSEGHEM PARK

Memories of the 1935 and 1958 Expos ...

Boulevard du Centenaire, avenue de l'Atomium
Metro and tram No. 23, 51, 84 and 88, Heysel stop

Little visited these days, the Osseghem Park is a charming if somewhat wild-looking expanse, spread across several different levels.

It also contains the vestiges of two Universal Expositions (1935 and 1958), including a magnificent open-air theatre, saved at the last minute from destruction.

Created on the site of a former sand quarry in preparation for the 1935 Exposition, it was conceived by Jules Buyssens along the lines of an English woodland park. A beautiful path with four rows of pruned copper beech trees leads into the grounds from place Louis Steens (corner of boulevard du Centenaire and avenue du Gros Tilleul). In the middle of the park two footbridges remain, one from 1935 and the other from 1958. At the north end stands a monument to the Belgian granite quarries, also dating from 1935.

In the wooded section around the Atomium, near the long winding pond, a tree has been poetically dedicated to the memory of the architect and landscape artist who created the park. Further into the woods, you'll come across the semicircular, terraced open-air theatre, also the work of Jules Buyssens (1935). The gravel, low stone walls, and golden privet hedges blend harmoniously with the natural setting and are a surprising contrast to the proud, gigantic balls of the nearby Atomium.

Two different eras, two different Expositions, and two different aesthetic doctrines confront one another here. The theatre, blessed with very good acoustics, was much used in both Expositions (for plays in 1935, brass bands and orchestras in 1958) and accommodated up to 3,000 spectators. It was then forgotten and it wasn't until 1997 that the city took charge of the site and listed it as a historic monument. Today, in summer, everyone can enjoy the magic intimacy of this theatre thanks to various festivals held here.

Don't forget to admire, alongside avenue de l'Atomium, the truncated dome covered in tiles of the former pavilion of the Comptoir Tuilier of Courtrai, one of the rare pavilions of the second Exposition still standing. Built by Guy Bontinck, it housed an exhibition on the history of tiles since Gallo-Roman times. Today converted into a restaurant, it's still a strange and futuristic wonder to behold.

Rue Mellery and rue des Vignes   ⑬

These two streets running alongside the royal park are vestiges of the original village of Laeken. They also attest to the expansionist appetite of the royal domain. If you examine the walls of the royal park, you'll notice that their appearance changes as you walk round: as the park was enlarged, it incorporated parts of the walls of the previous properties into that of the royal domain.

JARDINS DU FLEURISTE

A former property of Leopold II

Rue Médori, avenue des Robiniers and rue des Horticulteurs
Entrance by parc Sobieski, avenue Sobieski
02 775 75 11
jardinsdufleuriste.be
Information: Institut bruxellois pour la gestion de l'environnement (IBGE)
Metro Stuyvenberg

In addition to the Sobieski and Colonial parks, which both suffer from the proximity of traffic, you'll be delighted to discover another more isolated park perched on a hill and offering a splendid panoramic view of Brussels. This brand-new public park is intended 'to spread the arts and techniques of gardening.' It ingeniously combines attractive gardens with didactic spaces and cultural activities on a historic site. The grounds are composed of two parts separated by a steep slope. Below, greenhouses can be seen whose former splendour can only be imagined.

© Filharmoniker

Their future use hasn't yet been decided. The main part above contains planted areas, with various gardens offering different scenic paths and revealing some facets of the art of creating gardens.

The central axis of the park extends visually towards the centre of Brussels. The sustainable development philosophy underpins the whole project: a great diversity of vegetation, techniques of ecological gardening, and plants specific to certain times of the year, as well as many unfamiliar species, are all presented here on 4 hectares of land. This site once belonged to Leopold II (the grounds adjoined his Stuyvenberg estate) and formed, together with the Sobieski and Colonial parks, a zone devoted to horticulture, the royal orchards, and the acclimatization of species imported from the Belgian Congo. The works laying out the original gardens and greenhouses of Le Fleuriste were completed in 1900. When the grounds were transformed into public parks in the 1950s, these 4 hectares were not included and were gradually forgotten before being brought back to life in 2005.

FORMER WORKSHOP OF ERNEST SALU

Three generations of funerary artists

At the entrance to Laeken cemetery, parvis Notre Dame
Visits by arrangement: M. Celis, Epitaphe ASBL : 02 553 16 41 – epitaaf.org
Tram No. 94, Princesse Clémentine stop

Maintained by the members of Épitaphe, an association devoted to funerary archaeology, the former Salu workshop is an unusual place. This business was run from 1876 to 1983 by three generations of sculptors, passing from father to son, all of them bearing the same forename, Ernest.

The first Ernest Salu, 'the founder', was a graduate of the Académie Royale de Bruxelles, who gradually specialized in the art of creating funerary monuments. He himself drew up the plans in 1881 for the workshop and adjoining house, strategically situated next to the entrance to the Laeken cemetery. Naturally a number of his creations can be seen here. The enterprise was later reoriented by the founder's grandson towards restoration work, at a time when the demand for funerary monuments had drastically declined.

The existing entrance to the establishment leads to the winter garden, which dates from 1913. Very well preserved, its original function is obvious: the overhead lighting and mirrors highlight the sculptures on display. The moulding shop, where clay and plaster were worked, is particularly moving, as if the place had not been altered since the business closed down. Even the dust helps to prevent it from seeming too much like a museum.

The other spaces are filled with funerary sculptures, including some surprising bozettos (scaled-down studies of the tombs), models of hands and feet, and plaster castings. There is also a bust of Ernest Salu the First, along with great many documents, drawings and photos relating to funerary art.

On the first floor, the big bay windows look out on the cemetery and the funeral monument of the Salu family, deliberately placed at this spot. In fact it's a cenotaph, as no one is actually buried there.

NEARBY
Street Light Museum (16)
Rue Delva, between Rue Mabille and Rue Fineau

Sixteen *réverbères* (street lamps) from various periods (the date and origin of each lamp is indicated), are placed in chronological order in front of the Foyer Laekenois. Their presence provides a brief history of public lighting in Brussels: it was the first city on the European continent to equip itself with an urban lighting system. This heritage has generally not been preserved, however, and it's now rare to see the pieces gathered here. They thus let you appreciate the evolution not only in style but also in technology, with the major switch from gas to electricity. This display forms part of a larger project for incorporating works of art into groups of social housing.

CHOIR OF THE FORMER CHURCH ⑰ OF NOTRE-DAME DE LAEKEN

The last vestige of a 13th-century church

Laeken Cemetery
Parvis Notre-Dame de Laeken
Tuesday to Sunday and public holidays 8.30am–4.30pm
Tram No. 94, Princesse Clémentine stop
Metro Bockstael

© EmDee

There are very few visitors who notice the building in the middle of the Laeken Cemetery that now serves as a simple chapel. It is, however, the last vestige of the former church of Notre-Dame de Laeken and is associated with the choir of the former building.

While some sources claim it was consecrated by Pope Leo III when he passed through the region with Emperor Charlemagne in 803 or 804, or that it was founded in 895, or even in the 10th century, in reality it dates back to the 13th century.

In 1850, Louise-Marie d'Orléans (1812–1850), the first Queen of the Belgians and the wife of King Leopold I, was buried in a vault in the chapel of Sainte-Barbe, adjoining the left arm of the church's transept. The king then decided to have a new church built next door (the present-day Church of Our Lady of Laeken) in memory of his deceased wife.

After the consecration of the new church in 1872, only the choir remained, which was enclosed by a neo-Gothic façade and then moved to the nearby cemetery. It was listed in 1936.

When the Virgin destroyed the church walls four times

Legend has it that, three times, workmen found the church walls they had built the previous day had been knocked down. The guards, who were in charge of finding out the cause of this damage, saw the Virgin Mary (accompanied by Saint Barbara and Saint Catherine) descend from heaven and knock down the foundations of the church a fourth time. The Virgin then instructed them on the shape and size of the church and ordered the high altar to be placed not to the east, as was customary, but to the south. She gave them a thread that traced the layout of the church. The preciously preserved relic was stolen in 1633 by three deserters. Their leader, George Volmaer, was arrested and confessed under torture. He was flogged in front of the church and then taken to Brussels, where he was torn apart after having his right hand burnt.

NEARBY

The first copy of Rodin's The Thinker (18)

Among the many personalities buried here – including the likes of Fernand Khnopff, Josef Poelaert, La Malibran (a famous singer), Belliard, Bockstael and Delhaize – the tomb of art critic Josef Dillen, near the old entrance, is particularly noteworthy. It is decorated with the first copy of Rodin's famous sculpture, *The Thinker*.

Created in the 17th century, Brussels' oldest and most romantic cemetery soon attracted the aristocracy and bourgeoisie as it welcomed the burial place of the first Queen of the Belgians.

In 1857, as the population grew, Émile Bockstael suggested installing burial galleries. Niches were masoned into the high underground walls of the 1.5-hectare cemetery so that coffins could be inserted horizontally. Although access to the old galleries is forbidden due to their state of disrepair, the more recent section, which is open to the public, gives a slightly chilling impression.

Head towards the back of the cemetery to the imposing entrance, which dates from 1932, and take the staircase to the basement. One of the galleries extends far into the heart of the cemetery. A gate blocks the access, but the view gives a good idea of the extent of the network and the solemn, eternal atmosphere that emanates from it.

NEARBY

Passage Chambon

At the point where avenue de la Reine crosses the railway line, this small passage, not always indicated on city maps, possesses a certain charm despite its neglected state.

Located under the bridge constructed by architect A. Chambon in 1905, it lets pedestrians on avenue de la Reine cross beneath the tracks and reach rue Stiernet.

With its wrought-iron lamps, rose ceiling mouldings, vases, and balustrades in Belgian bluestone, the furnishing of this little byway is particularly appealing.

Brasserie Le Royal
Parvis Notre-Dame de Laeken 11

This former Art Deco bakery is now home to a delightful brasserie that is a perfect echo to the royal crypt. Its walls are filled with a multitude of royal portraits, some of which are quite conventional while others are one-of-a-kind, like that depicting Prince Baudouin as a boy scout.

The welcoming wooden panelling is cleverly made from salvaged pieces of Art Deco beds. The prices are very democratic despite the resolutely monarchic ambiance.

ROYAL CRYPT

A largely unsung site of Belgian royalty

Church of Notre-Dame de Laeken
Parvis Notre-Dame de Laeken
Every Sunday 2pm–5pm

Since 1834, the reigning Belgian sovereigns and their wives, along with certain members of the Belgian royal family, have been buried in the Royal Crypt of the Church of Notre-Dame de Laeken. Unknown to many Belgians (the church is open one day a week), it is a solemn, sober, and rather gloomy place.

The origin of this tradition goes back to the first Queen of the Belgians, Louise-Marie d'Orléans, who, although she died in Ostend in 1850, wished to be buried in Laeken. Her wish was respected, and her body was laid to rest for several years in the former church of Laeken (of which only the choir remains today, in the Laeken cemetery, see previous double page).

Her husband, King Leopold I, felt the place was not worthy of the royal family and ordered the construction of a new, large church in Laeken. Built by Joseph Poelaert in the neo-Gothic style, the church was consecrated in 1872, although it was not completed until 1909.

Twenty-one royals are buried there, including five kings (Leopold I, Leopold II, Albert I, Leopold III and Baudouin), five queens and one empress (Charlotte of Belgium, Empress of Mexico, wife of Emperor Maximilian I of Mexico and daughter of Leopold I).

In 1876, the remains of King Leopold I, Queen Louise-Marie and Prince Leopold were transferred from the vault of the old Laeken church to the vault of the new church (see illustration).

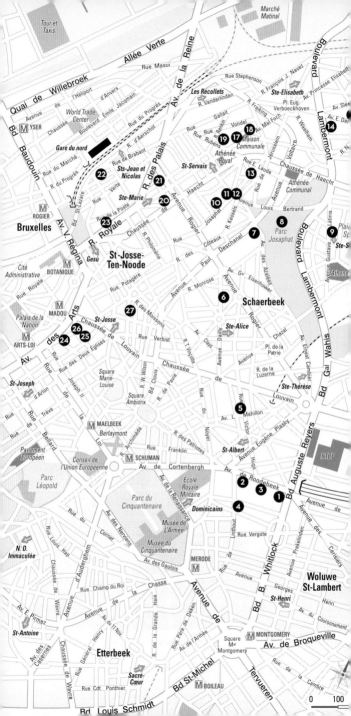

Schaerbeek, Saint-Josse-ten-Noode

THE CLOCKARIUM

Chock-a-block with clocks

Boulevard Reyers 163
02 732 08 28 – clockarium.com
Every Sunday
Guided tours only, at 3.05pm (duration about 1 h 20 min)
Trams No. 23, 24 or 25, Diamant stop

The Clockarium is an unusual private museum with a collection of faience clocks from the inter-war period. Installed in a beautiful Art Deco house, it displays a selection of 1,300 pieces out of a total of 3,200.

Why faience clocks? Quite simply because the present curator, Jacques de Selliers, a former manager for Solvay, started to become interested in them and to haunt second-hand shops looking for these objects, now somewhat neglected and very often forgotten in the corner of people's attics. It took him only a decade to acquire this astonishing collection, the equivalent of almost one clock a day.

If his buying rate has today slowed down considerably, he is still enthusiastic enough to lead guided tours of his personal museum. And that's what makes it so interesting.

In the 1920s, the clock was still a relatively luxury item and the sign of a certain success in life. It was considered good form to place one on the mantelpiece, the central feature in living rooms at the time. This tradition was mainly found in France and Belgium: the Germanic countries heated their homes principally with stoves and fireplaces were uncommon. Further to the south, there was less need for fireplaces, and in England, people preferred tall wooden clocks. But in France and Belgium, faience clocks were favoured, being both cheap and decorative.

You'll notice that all the clocks in the museum are stopped at 10 past 10, as they are in all shops selling timepieces. The impression given by this raised position of the hour and minute hands, is simply thought to be more positive than if they were pointing downwards at 4.40, much more discouraging!

Faience

Ceramic is a generic term used to designate an object made from clay (*keramon* in Greek) that has been fired. Faience is the most simple form of ceramic and probably the most widespread.

Its name comes from the Italian town of Faenza, which began large-scale production of ceramics in the 15th century.

Higher up the quality scale (in terms of delicacy and transparency) there is china, then porcelain, whose raw materials, other than clay, also include kaolin.

A taste for beauty with civic values

Avenue de Roodebeek 61 et 103
02 734 34 63
Open during class hours
Trams No. 23, 24 or 25, Diamant stop

© Jean-Jacques Evrard

Less well-known than the school complex in rue Josaphat, the Linthout School Complex is nonetheless a magnificent Art Nouveau construction by the architect Henri Jacobs, with the help of Maurice Langaskcns at No. 103 and Privat Livemont at No. 61. If you ask at the entrance, you can visit this site when students are in class.

Initially conceived to house two linked primary schools, with the boys being taught at No. 103 and the girls at No. 61, today it also comprises School No. 13 and the extension to the Athénée Fernand Blum. At No. 103, inaugurated in 1913, a small hallway leads to a first pretty courtyard that opens onto the façade of the covered yard, slightly masked by trees. Once you find yourself in this covered yard, decorated in the Art Nouveau style, a sense of lightness fills you. A vast well-ventilated space with a glass ceiling overhead and a splendid fresco on the rear wall: *L'étude* (Study) recounting a scene from *Contes de l'ancêtre* (The Ancestor's Tales) and another representing a *Berger étudiant les étoiles* (Shepherd Studying the Stars). The local authorities at the time sought to give students a taste for beauty while instilling them with civic values.

A short distance from there, No. 61 is built according to the same principles and with an almost identical spatial arrangement. It was inaugurated in 1922, nine years later than No. 103 due to the outbreak of the First World War: during the occupation, the Germans requisitioned steel for making reinforced concrete. You'll discover another vast covered yard here, with a large and beautiful fresco. Painted by Privat Livemont, it recalls the values of 'Primary Education' as well as 'Study and Work'. As you leave the inner courtyard, open the door to the right. The hallway leading to the gymnasium contains several magnificent sgraffiti, unfortunately deteriorated, also by Privat Livemont. And take a look at the gymnasium itself and its handsome Art Nouveau ceiling, with graceful, refined curves.

NEARBY

Cité ouvrière de Linthout ③

Access at Rue Général Gratry 84–88 and by avenue de Roodebeek
A pretty estate of small houses with gardens. The approach from avenue Général Gratry is more interesting, notably for the unusual view of the central house in the estate. Look out for the small vegetable garden to the left of this house.

Rue de Linthout 88 ④

At the corner of rue Victor-Lefèvre. A building with pretty sgraffiti signed by Gustave Strauven.

LES CONTES DE L'ANCÊTRE

BERGERS ÉTUDIANT LES ÉTOILES

FAÇADE OF THE FOYER SCHAERBEEKOIS

'Be active, be clean, be thrifty, for everyone'

Rue Victor Hugo 53–59

© Michel Wal

At the end of the 19th century, several municipalities across Brussels embarked on vast social housing construction programmes aimed at the poor. Slums in unhealthy cul-de-sacs were demolished and local authorities bought the land.

The municipality of Schaerbeek, which was particularly wealthy at the end of the century, built many of these housing estates, some of which have now been demolished.

The two buildings at No. 55 Rue Victor Hugo were designed by architect Henri Jacobs (who also built around 15 school buildings – see p. 272) in an eclectic style with a strong Art Nouveau influence.

The flats, built in 1899, consisted of three rooms with running water and flushing toilets, and were considered very luxurious at the time. They were saved from destruction in 1968 and eventually renovated in 2001. The flats that were deemed too small for today's standards were merged.

The yellow, orange, red and black brick facades have been remarkably restored, including the beautiful sgraffiti that celebrate, in French and Dutch, the values of living together, cleanliness, hard work and frugality.

The typically Art Nouveau arabesques under the cornices are also noteworthy.

The central bay has been completely preserved, with its original frames, columns, and colour. While the entrance doors have been changed, the original wrought iron oculus with the letters F and S for 'Foyer Schaerbeekois' has been replaced.

This is a fine example of a restoration carried out without the use of new materials, which would not have been in keeping with the original, and it shows how considered social housing was more than a century ago.

THE HOUSE OF CATS

6

Whether it's dark or not, all cats are blue

Avenue Dailly 48

I n front of No. 48 Avenue Dailly, you have to cross the road and look up to admire the magnificent ceramic frieze at the top of the building.

It features five blue cats in a perfectly symmetrical arrangement. On either side, two cats have their backs turned as they stare at the trio in

he centre, who gaze at passers-by while exuding a rather hostile attitude.

Built in 1901 by the Franco-Belgian architect Alban Chambon, the ouse is a blend of eclectic and Art Nouveau styles.

The cats are reminiscent of the famous poster *Tournée du Chat Noir e Rodolphe Salis,* designed by Théophile Steinlen and published in rance in 1896.

Could that have been where Chambon went for entertainment and nspiration?

ELECTRIC MAST

7

A vestige of the 1913 Ghent Universal Exhibition

Roundabout between avenues Louis Bertrand and Paul Deschanel

There is a curious Art Nouveau metal structure that occasionall catches the eye of curious passers-by on the roundabout that join the avenues Louis Bertrand and Paul Deschanel.

Few people know that this large mast, originally designed in plaster

was exhibited at the Brussels Salon in 1887, where it caused a sensation. Its creator, the sculptor Jacques de Lalaing, dreamt of seeing his work incorporated into the public space. In 1888, there were talks of placing the mast in Square Ambiorix, a major Art Nouveau site (see p. 110).

In 1893, it was suggested that the structure should be placed in front of the monumental Gare du Midi train station, and the following year on the Place de Brouckère.

In the end, the final bronze version was installed at the Ghent Universal Exhibition in 1913, opposite the Congo pavilion. A year later, the war drove it into a warehouse.

In 1926, the sculptor's heirs offered the electric mast to the Schaerbeek municipality which had it placed at the entrance to Josaphat Park. There, it stood proudly until 1953, when roadworks meant there was no more room for it. Once again it was stored in a municipal warehouse and was moved in 1993, to stand in front of the majestic Maison Communale de Schaerbeek on Place Colignon, without its lights.

In 2006, it was finally returned to its original location, where it stands today. It was restored in 2013 and regained its missing lights.

With its triangular base, this 15-metre-high mast is topped by a lighting system in a style steeped in Art Nouveau, which is both a work of art and street furniture.

Don't hesitate to cross the circular walkway to reach the base of this work of art, where you can admire up close the three sides of the high-relief at the base of the mast, depicting a titanic battle between tigers and snakes against a backdrop of banana leaves.

GAND
1913

Le Pavillon du Congo
De Congoleesche Afdeeling
Kolonialpalast
The Pavilion of the belgian Congo

BAR-RESTAURANT OF THE ROYAL GUILD OF SAINT SEBASTIAN

The archers shoot at clay pigeons suspended from poles about 20 m high

Parc Josaphat. Upper part
Bar-restaurant open from mid-March to beginning of November, depending on the weather, from 11am–9pm/10pm
Archery sessions: from May to October, every Friday at 6.30pm
Bus No. 66, Azalées stop, or tram No. 23, Héliotropes stop

The oldest archery association in the Parc Josephat (named after the valley near Jerusalem), the Guilde de Saint-Sébastien owns a bar-restaurant in front of the targets.

You can have a pleasant time there watching the training sessions and competitions. The archers shoot in a rather spectacular fashion at clay pigeons suspended from poles (or perches) about 20 m high. The central part of the park is thus totally emptied during competitions, and when training the archers are isolated by giant screens at the foot of the poles to prevent arrows falling on walkers.

This tradition dates back to the 16th century, when the guild was founded: each year, archers shot at the bird from the spire of the nearby Saint-Servais church. The winner was proclaimed king of the guild and received three insignia: a necklace strung with silver plaques, a ceremonial baton, and a silver bird of honour. After a third consecutive victory, the archer was solemnly named emperor. One of the guild's banners is visible on the stairs leading to the first floor of the Schaerbeek Municipal Hall. St Sebastian has been the patron saint of archers since the 4th century. He is also the patron of the Guilde des Archers de Bruxelles, and for this reason his image is found on the tympanum of the door

© Guilde Saint-Sébastien

to the tower of the Hôtel de Ville.

A painting by Memling depicts *The Martyrdom of St Sebastian* at the Museum of Ancient Art.

St Sebastian

Probably born in Milan, Sebastian enlisted in the Roman army around AD 283. Appointed captain of the Praetorian Guard by Emperor Diocletian, he soon drew attention to himself due to his Christian faith and proselytizing activities. Arrested, he was sentenced to die pierced with arrows by his own soldiers. But the latter took care to aim only at non-fatal areas of their former chief's body. Left for dead at the foot of the post to which he was attached, it was finally Irene, the widow of St Castulus, who found him still alive and treated his wounds. Once healed, Sebastian posted himself where Diocletian would pass in order to proclaim his faith. Exasperated by his insolence, the emperor ordered him to be stoned and his body dumped into the Roman sewer (*cloaca maxima*). After he was canonized, it was claimed that he had the power to halt the plague: in 680 when an epidemic was ravaging Rome, his relics were taken out in a procession and the plague ceased.

SAINTE-SUZANNE CHURCH

The concrete-built church shades harmoniously from pink to brown in typical Art Deco style

Avenue Gustave Latinis 66
Mass daily at 6.30pm, Friday at 9am, Saturday at 5pm, and Sunday at 10am
Tram No. 23, Louis Bertrand stop, bus No. 66

A short walk from boulevard Lambermont, Sainte-Suzanne is a remarkable church built in Art Deco style, which also possesses magnificent contemporary stained-glass windows. Of the three concrete-built churches in Brussels, Sainte-Suzanne is the oldest (the other two are Saint-Augustin at place de l'Altitude 100 in Forest, and Saint-Jean-Baptiste in Molenbeek). The church was constructed mainly thanks to funds from the widow of General Maes, who had lost her only daughter Suzanne in 1914, at the age of 20. The parish naturally adopted the name desired by its benefactress and the church celebrated its first rites on 11 August 1928, the feast day of St Suzanne. A niece of Pope Caius, she was decapitated during the persecutions of Diocletian around the year 300.

© Jean-Jacques Evrard

From the outside, the building is striking with its concrete frame and its bell tower rising in successive stages to a height of 49 m. Characteristic of Art Deco, it uses several palettes of colour, shading harmoniously from pink to ochre or to brown. Its architect, Jean Combaz, was inspired by the church at Raincy in the Paris suburbs, built by August Perret. The interior, which can hold up to 1,000 people, is surprisingly vast.

For the first time in Belgium, the use of concrete allowed the construction of a single nave, without any columns or pillars. To the right as you enter, note the pretty baptistery created in 1935 by the Maredsous art workshops. On the floor, you'll see mosaics in black, yellow and red, a reminder of the military career and patriotism of Madame Maes's husband. Nevertheless, it is the stained glass that does most to enhance the church's artistic worth: composed of six large windows, they are all the work of the same artist (Simon Steger) and the same master glassmaker (Jacques Colpaert). Each of the windows is decorated by stained glass on the inside, and a novelty at the time, clear glass on the outside. This provided better insulation and also better protection against the effects of pollution. Extremely luminous today, Sainte-Suzanne was originally even more so: when it was first built, a seventh window was placed behind the altar and the caisson ceiling had nine skylights in the form of a cross. But as it was then thought that religious contemplation required dim light, all these windows were removed.

© Jean-Jacques Evrard

COMMUNITY SCHOOL NO.1

The almost perfect example of an ideal school

Rue Josaphat 229–241 and Rue de la Ruche 30
Open during class hours
Tram No. 92, Saint-Servais stop

The school at rue Josaphat and rue de la Ruche in Schaerbeek is probably the most beautiful example in Brussels of Art Nouveau applied to school architecture. As in the case of most schools in the city, they'll probably let you have a quiet look around during class if you ask tactfully. Although there is an entrance on rue de la Ruche, the main entrance is in rue Josephat.

Inaugurated on 6 October 1907, the École Primaire No. 1 is the most famous building by the local Schaerbeek architect Henri Jacobs. Full of praise at the time, the review *La Ligue des architectes* spoke of 'the almost perfect example of an ideal school.'

Initially containing 24 classrooms in all, with a nursery school, a primary school for boys, another for girls, and a technical school, the complex made an impact due to the quality of its facilities: gymnasium, swimming pool, library and several open-air playgrounds. Nothing was too good for this project costing over 2 million Belgian francs, a considerable budget at the time. *La Ligue des architectes* even wondered whether 'it was not too much luxury being spent on children: we are of the opinion that simplicity should be the first concern of the author when designing a work of this nature.'

But beyond the wealth of its amenities, Jacobs, who was a disciple of Hankar, carried out a veritable work of art here, both in terms of architecture and of decor.

Created by Privat Livemont, numerous sgraffiti are to be found within the building, which explains why, protected from the weather, they are in such a rare state of preservation: the colours are for the most part original. For his motifs, Privat Livemont was partly inspired by local history. You thus find the donkey of Schaerbeek and beehives, which allude to both the name of the local street and to bees, synonymous with hard work.

© Jean-Jacques Evrard

CERAMICS FROM THE FORMER SAINT-SERVAIS CHURCH

The Bacchanalian vase on the site of the choir of the former church of the old village of Schaerbeek

Avenue Louis Bertrand 53–61

© Jean-Jacques Evrard

Listed in 2008, the remarkable group of houses at Nos. 53–61 was designed by architect Gustave Strauven. Above Strauven's handsome signature, under the restaurant's awning, is a beautiful ceramic panel depicting the former Saint Servais church, which was destroyed when Avenue Louis Bertrand was built. Above, another ceramic panel shows a donkey's head surrounded by cherries (the emblem of Schaerbeek). Both ceramics are marked 'céramiques Wezel, 16 rue Kessels'.

The Bacchanal vase, a work by Godefroid Devresse in the centre of Avenue Louis Bertrand, stands on the site of the choir of the old church.

The construction of the new avenue resulted in the destruction of the centre of the village of Schaerbeek around the old Saint-Servais church, which had been disused since 1876 but was only demolished in 1905. The former Gothic-style church was the heart of the Schaerbeek village. The two Saint-Servais churches (the old one, now demolished, and the current one) coexisted for around 30 years.

At No. 10 Avenue Louis Bertrand are beautiful, albeit very faded, sgraffiti.

NEARBY
Shoe scraper from the Verhaeghe house ⑫

At No. 43, the Maison Verhaeghe, also designed by Gustave Strauven (1906), was listed in 2006. There you can admire an Art Nouveau-style shoe scraper.

© Michel Wal

HOUSE AND STUDIO
OF THE PAINTER RUYTINX

*A beautiful, little-known sgraffito, an allegory of
painting*

Rue Vogler 17

Built in 1906 for the painter Alfred Ruytinx by an unidentified
architect, the house at 17 rue Vogler boasts a beautiful sgraffito
created by Privat Livemont, the artist's uncle. Restored in a rather
unfortunate fashion in 1992 by the present owner, despite the latter
being a retired art teacher, the sgraffito has today lost some of its
original colours. The contrasts between shades are now too sharp, and
are accentuated by the light grey paint of the façade. But the charming
original drawing is nevertheless still visible. An allegory of the art of

© Jean-Jacques Evrard

painting in honour of the original owner, it represents a woman holding a palette and brush, as well as an infant, surrounded by a sea of greenery, chestnut leaves and buds.

NEARBY

Boulevard Lambermont 146 and 150

Two beautiful examples of Art Nouveau houses with restored sgraffiti. At No. 168 there are more sgraffiti, but they are badly deteriorated.

Avenue Eugène Demolder ⑮

A fine-looking avenue lined with some pretty houses. No. 4 has a poorly preserved sgraffito, No. 8 built by Leemans in 1911 has several sgraffiti and an interesting rounded form, while No. 24 was designed by François Hemelsoet. Note the metalwork at the top of the building here, which is rather reminiscent of the Musical Instruments Museum. Lastly, at No. 27, there are some more beautiful sgraffiti.

MOERASKE

A green motorway

Rue de la Perche (Evère)
Free entry except for Parc Walckiers (tours only)
Free guided tour every second Sunday of the month at 10am, or an à la carte
visit for €50 (group of maximum 20) by calling 02 242 50 43
Bus No. 45, 54, 59 or 69, Église Saint-Vincent stop

It was the 20th-century love affair with motorways that would paradoxically lead to the creation of Le Moeraske park and its peculiar elongated shape (almost 2 km long): this spot, today filled with birds, aquatic areas and wild vegetation, was earmarked for the motorway from Antwerp.

The land was therefore bought up by compulsory purchase, the projected route filled in with rubbish and earth, and the water flowing from nearby springs collected in a pond. But the motorway plans were eventually abandoned and nature was once again allowed to take its course. The regulating pond became a marsh (*moeraske* is Flemish for 'little marsh'), the filled-in area was metamorphosed into Parc du Bon-

© Omondi

Pasteur and Parc Walckiers returned to a wild state. Strangely enough, all this upheaval has given rise to a site of extraordinary biological wealth and diversity: wetlands, drylands, woodlands, a stream (the Kerkebeek), springs, marshes and vegetable gardens.

The site also bears witness to local history. In the north-east, you'll find an old water tower that once fed the boilers of steam locomotives in the nearby train station: the park's 14 hectares are in fact next to the marshalling yards at Schaerbeek. The enormous watering stopcock is still visible along the railway line. An old advertisement, at No. 44 rue Walckiers, recalls the existence of companies offering insurance against war damage. A former bomb shelter can also be seen at the corner of rue Carli and rue du Château.

Threatened successively by development projects promoted by the Belgian railway company (SNCB) and the Schaerbeek commune, this zone has fortunately been defended by local residents mobilizing to protect a park that has become dear to their hearts. For some, the possibility of simply watching the trains go by, sitting in the long grass, has become a rare pleasure so close to the city centre.

It's also ideal for families with children.

SCHAERBEEK
MUNICIPAL HALL

Very few entered it

Place Colignon

© Edison McCullen

f most Brussels residents know the imposing Schaerbeek Municipal Hall, very few have ever been inside. Built out in the countryside by the architect Jules Jacques Van Ysendick, then reconstructed in 1911 after a fire, this town hall is a good example of Flemish neo-Renaissance style. Admire above all the stained-glass windows of the main stairway inside, the two lateral staircases, the glass wall at the rear and the principal rooms at the front of the building, notably the wedding hall and the council chambers. The chambers have some pretty Malines tapestries representing cherry trees, whose fruit is the symbol of this commune.

© Edison McCullen

NEARBY

Private house of Henri Jacobs (18)

Avenue Maréchal Foch 9

A short distance from the Schaerbeek Municipal Hall, the architect Henri Jacobs built a house in 1903 that served as both his residence and office. It has in particular a magnificent sgraffito between the cornice and the four ogival windows on the upper floor. It owes its good state of conservation to the wide overhang of the cornice, which has protected it from the elements. This same cornice, however, has the drawback of leaving the top of the sgraffito in shadow much of the time. As you walk by, admire the neighbouring house at No. 11, also built by Jacobs. Henri Jacobs was also architect of the schools in rue Josaphat and avenue de Roodebeek, as well as the Institut Diderot at Les Marolles.

FRANS VAN OPHEM HOUSE

An unsung beauty

Rue Renkin 33
Metro Gare-du-Nord
Cannot be visited, but visible from the road

© Jean-Jacques Evrard

I t was in 1897 that architect and entrepreneur Frans Van Ophem built his remarkable private house at Rue Renkin 33.

Eclectic in style, it features Art Nouveau elements such as the magnificent sgraffiti on the right-hand side illustrating the building trades, and the architect's stylised signature on the metal plate of the letterbox (also in Art Nouveau style).

A fine bas-relief (signed V. De Haen) overlooks the ground-floor window, to the left of the entrance door. It depicts a reclining woman, with the dome of the Sainte-Marie church in Schaerbeek in the background.

Renovated in 2003 in keeping with the original design, the house is privately owned and cannot be visited.

Renkin, by the way, is the pseudonym of Rennequin, born in 1645 and famous for having built a pumping system at Marly-le-Roy during the reign of Louis XIV, designed to bring the waters of the Seine to the ponds at Versailles, 119 m higher.

© Jean-Jacques Evrard

NEARBY

Several other homes on rue Renkin have interesting features. A little further on, at No. 72, and despite the lack of any sign, stands the Espace Géo de Vlamynck, named after the Belgian artist whose studio can be seen nearby in rue de la Constitution (see p. 288).

The house in this street can be visited as part of the Géo de Vlamynck tour, on the second Sunday of every month. Next door at No. 74, you'll be surprised to learn that the architect of this handsome townhouse is none other than Paul Saintenoy.

Its style is very different from the former Old England department store in Brussels, which has now become the Musical Instruments Museum. This house was built in 1911 for the painter Frans Kegeljan, the rich heir of a banking family from Namur. At No. 90, you'll also notice an Art Nouveau house with sgraffiti.

GARDEN OF THE MAISON DES ARTS GASTON WILLIOT

An unexpected garden of delights

Chaussée de Haecht 147
Trams No. 92 or 95, bus No. 65 or 66, Robiano stop

The Maison des Arts Gaston Williot is a little-known gem of a house at Schaerbeek and the only patrician dwelling in the commune dating back before 1830. It greets visitors with its Louis XV and Louis XVI salons, some pretty stained-glass windows that have managed to survive intact, and a magnificent garden. This is in principle reserved to women with young children, but in practice others can go in most of the time. You'll then have a view of a rectangular lawn decorated with a few statues. Sit down on one of the benches, breathe in deeply,

and appreciate the contrast with the surrounding busy streets in a neighbourhood lacking green spaces. The surprising roof made of steel and glass seen to one side of the garden is that of the Schaerbeek market.

The Maison des Arts was originally the home of a rich Brussels draper, Charles Louis Eenens, who had it built in 1826. The property then passed to his elder son, General Eenens, who engaged in a long dispute with the commune due to the expropriation of the large garden which was blocking the construction of rue Royale Sainte-Marie. Bought by the commune in 1950 and listed as a historic building in 1993, the Maison des Arts today hosts artistic events such as the Biennale de la Sculpture. It also regularly puts on exhibitions open to the general public. The Maison des Arts owes much of its success to Gaston Williot, bourgmestre of Schaerbeek from 1963 to 1971. It was Williot who pushed forward with restoration and other major improvements to the house.

The most remarkable feature is probably the delftware mantelpiece graced with manganese squares. André Maurois, Jean Cocteau, Michel Simon, and Jacques Brel were just some of the famous visitors here. Before that, the crown prince of the Netherlands in 1830 and Hermann Goering in 1917 both stayed here. Prince Frederick of Nassau, head of the Dutch forces occupying Belgium at the time, even set up his headquarters in the library during the revolutionary events of 1830. It was here that he decided to withdraw his troops towards Antwerp, once faced with armed patriots who had gathered in the Parc de Bruxelles. In memory of this historic moment, the cup from which the prince drank his tea that day, 26 September, has been preserved. The façades were restored in 1994. Don't forget to have a look at the little 1900-style café in the chateau's former saddle room.

© Alfred de Ville de Goyet

GÉO DE VLAMYNCK STUDIO AND WALKING TOUR

You'd think the artist had just gone out for a moment

Rue de la Constitution 7
02 215 01 26
geodevlamynck.be
Tours every second Sunday of the month, at 2.30pm
Meeting point at the Halles de Schaerbeek
Duration of tour: 3 h
Trams No. 92 and 94, or train to Gare du Nord

The tour of sites associated with the artist Géo de Vlamynck (not to be confused with Maurice de Vlaminck, the celebrated French Fauvist painter) starts with his former studio. Preserved intact, it is a superb example of a 19th-century artist's studio, the oldest to be found in Brussels after that of Antoine Wiertz. It has a warm, cosy atmosphere, as if the artist had just gone out for a moment and was about to return: there are documents spread out on the desk, jars of pigment on a little shelf, and frames stacked in a corner ready for use. An old stove with a blackened pipe sits in the middle of the room.

Danielle de Vlamynck, the artist's daughter, then invites visitors to take a little walk through Schaerbeek to the Neptunium pool at place de Houffalize. It was there in 1957 that Vlamynck created a monumental mosaic, 2 m by 15 m. Lastly, you go to 72 rue Rankin where the Association des Amis de Géo de Vlamynck is based. Over a drink, Madame de Vlamynck will show you other works by her father, with frescoes and canvasses adorning the walls of an entire floor in this house.

Géo de Vlamynck (*Bruges 1897 – Brussels 1980*)

Géo de Vlamynck moved to Brussels in 1919 to escape from the artistic dullness that held sway in the city of his birth and hindered his creativity. He became the student of Constant Montald who would influence him considerably. In 1921, he won the Grand Prix de Rome for his painting, *The Repentant Sinner*. It was in 1924 that he bought the studio in rue de la Constitution. Built in 1862 for the sculptor De Hane, the house was later occupied by a number of artists, including the Impressionist painter from Schaerbeek, Eugène Smits. Exercising his talents in the different domains of painting, mosaics, stained glass with works such as *Marie mother of Christ at the Lake Shore* at the Koekelberg basilica, frescoes (including those carried out with his pupil Nicolas de Staël for the 1935 Universal Exposition in Brussels), and ceramics, Vlamynck is famous above all for his female nudes.

© Sylvie Olivier

BUNKER CINÉ-THÉÂTRE

Bar and trash concerts for curious night owls

Rue des Plantes 66A
Contact the owner, Patrice, on 02 223 34 59
bunker-cine-theatre.wifeo.com
Film club, theatre, occasional concerts
Metro Rogier

Located right in the middle of the red-light district around the Gare du Nord, practically between two display windows with prostitutes lit up in pink and mauve neon, the Bunker Ciné is an off-beat place likely to please the curious night owl. Like the Nova cinema, it truly deserves its name with its post-industrial decor, but it is even more 'underground' in flavour than its cousin in the city centre.

Although from time to time it organizes film club evenings, the Bunker Ciné is really more than just a cinema: it also occasionally hosts concerts that tend towards the harder, trashier end of the rock spectrum, which, beyond the quality of the music itself, do give the crowd the chance to let it all hang all out. Given the loud volume, you can scream and shout as loud as you please, as a means of relaxation after a hard day at work.

After this little session in anti-stress therapy, be sure to admire the old photo developing machines that sit by the entry to the main room. The Bunker is in fact installed in a former photographic laboratory built in the 1930s, which Patrice, the present owner, first cleared out and then lovingly renovated.

You should next head for the bar, whose atmosphere of relative calm is a welcome relief from the concert hall. Exhibiting the same brutal style, the decor here also takes up the theme of photography. A display case presents various bits of film, and old strips of the stuff are lying around in a corner. You feel strangely at ease as, beer in hand, you watch the world go by in these slightly surreal surroundings. But as is often the case in this type of place in Brussels, the customers and the boss here are absolutely adorable.

NEARBY

Le Royal building (23)

Rue Royale 284
Open during office hours

Like a beacon overlooking the street from the top of its vertical strip of yellow light, this building at 284 rue Royale is a fine example of Art Deco architecture. Constructed between 1936 and 1938 to plans drawn up by Jos Duijnstee, this project was a commission from Rotterdamse Verzekering Societeiten (RVS), which was celebrating its centenary in 1938. The entrance hall is the main attraction with its handsome floor mosaics, stained glass, and a very pretty ceramic panel recalling RVS's first hundred years. But the conference room on the first floor also has mosaics as well as another panel of ceramic tiles representing a hunting scene. If in theory visits should be booked in advance, you'll probably be allowed to look around simply by asking.

SAINTE-JULIENNE CHURCH

A forgotten church

Rue de la Charité 41
Metro Madou

Sainte-Julienne is a very beautiful church built in neo-Gothic style, but invisible from the street. Walking down rue de la Charité, No. 41 seems be just another block of flats, with the ground floor apparently forming part of the Caritas offices whose entrance is located at No. 43. Nothing indicates the existence of one of the most splendid churches in Brussels. It is only by going around the corner to 2 rue du Marteau, that you can see, if the gate is open, part of the church and a bit of the former cloister of the Congrégation des Religieuses de Sainte-Julienne. Built between 1883 and 1886, the church is a very handsome example of neo-Gothic architecture and decorated with mural paintings illustrating highlights of the life of St Julienne. The interior of the church is unfortunately no longer accessible since it was purchased and renovated by the Brussels Region. Its future use has yet to be decided.

St Julienne and the Fête-Dieu

Born in 1192 near Liège, St Julienne had a revelation at the age of 18 that would transform her life: God had charged her with establishing within the Roman Catholic Church the feast of the Holy Sacrament or *Fête-Dieu*. For 20 years, she believed herself to be unworthy of this mission. But having become the mother superior of the Abbaye de Cornillon, she once again received a revelation with the clear instruction to act without delay. After many difficulties, the first Holy Sacrament was finally celebrated at Liège in 1247 before becoming an official Catholic holiday in 1264. Held on the Thursday following the first Sunday after Pentecost, the *Fête-Dieu*, or feast of the Body of Christ (called Corpus Christi in some countries), expresses gratitude to God for having offered man the symbol of the Eucharist or the host as the Body of Christ.

© Andreas Praefcke

NEARBY
Rue du Vallon 22–28 ㉕

These houses, in very poor condition today, were designed by the architect Léon Sneyers in 1903 in a geometric Art Nouveau style. They have some fine ceramic tiled scenes.

CONCERTS AT
THE CHARLIER MUSEUM

Classical music by candlelight

Avenue des Arts 16
02 218 53 82 – 02 220 26 90 – charliermuseum.be
Monday to Thursday 12pm–5pm and Friday 10am–1pm
Guided tours may be booked (02 220 28 19) for groups of 15 persons maximum
Metro Madou

The Charlier Museum is an intimate museum, run with great enthusiasm by its present curator, Francine Delépine. She has preserved the generous spirit of mutual aid advocated by the museum's founders and still organizes a number of events there in support of charitable causes. Madame Delépine has also taken the happy initiative of arranging classical musical concerts of very high quality, offering moments of real pleasure and harmony, especially when these evening sessions take place by candlelight.

The museum itself is located in a handsome 19th-century townhouse that was the residence of the Brussels art lover and patron Henri van Cutsem. In order to exhibit his collections, he had his private house refurbished by the young architect Victor Horta in 1890. There are few traces of the Art Nouveau style, however, as Horta was not yet the great master he would later become. On his death in 1904, van Cutsem left the building to the sculptor Charlier (1854–1925) for whom he felt great affection. Following in the steps of his benefactor, Charlier

© DR

began to collect the work of contemporary Belgian artists. When he in turn died, the townhouse with all its collections were bequeathed to the commune of Saint-Josse-ten-Noode on condition that it become a museum. It opened its doors in 1928.

Today a rich variety of collections are preserved in welcoming surroundings. There are paintings by 19th- and 20th-century Belgian artists (Ensor, Vogels, Boulenger, etc.), sculptures by Charlier, of course, as well as by Rik Wouters, furniture and objects of decorative art in the styles of Louis XV, Louis XVI and the Empire, Belgian gold and silver plate, along with tapestries made in Brussels and Aubusson. Don't miss the Credo on the first floor.

© Andreas Praefcke

NEARBY
Govaerts House ㉗
Rue de Liederkerke 112

Built in 1860 in an eclectic style, this house was bought in 1899 by architect Léon Govaerts, who also happens to be responsible for the town hall of Saint-Josse commune. He proceeded to make drastic modifications to the building, giving it pretty multicoloured decorations inspired by the Art Nouveau style, still visible today. Purchased in 1995 and renovated by the commune, at present it is occupied by a recreation centre for the elderly, as well as by the Maison de la Famille. If you ring at the door, the people in charge will usually let you see some of the interior decor and notably the main staircase.

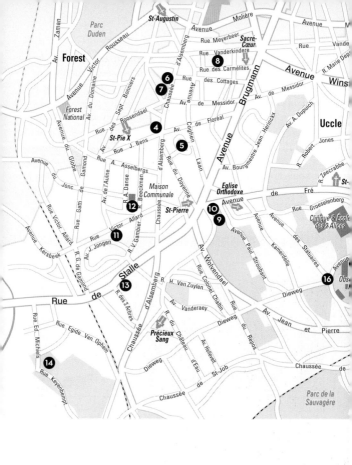

Uccle

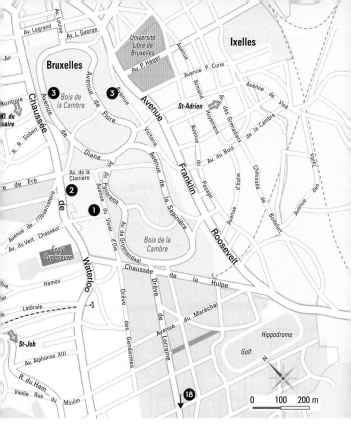

ROYAL ÉTRIER BELGE

Take tea at a private equestrian ring

Champ du Vert Chasseur 19
Club House : 02 374 38 70
royaletrierbelge.be
Daily except Monday
Kitchen: 9am–8pm
Bus No. 41 Vert chasseur stop

The Etrier ring, located beyond Bois de la Cambre park, near Uccle, is the prototype of a socialite country club.

Designed in 1929–1930 by architect Gaston Ide, this equestrian school was created at the initiative of the Solvay family in order to provide an equestrian centre for the officers, aristocracy and members of the upper middle class of Brussels. Inspired by the Flemish neo-Renaissance style, which is characterized by woodwork and ironwork painted in green and red, the complex is both very elegant and completely surreal, given that the Grand-Place is just a 10-minute drive away.

The neighbourhood of the Royal Etrier is also worth a visit. The Vert Chasseur district, which is rather secluded and only lightly urbanized, is a neighbourhood like no other. This little village, which was originally grouped around chaussée de Waterloo, was urbanized rather recently. In 1864, after the City of Brussels developed the Bois de la Cambre park, a part of the Vert Chasseur district was annexed to Brussels despite the fact that it was an inclusive part of Uccle territory.

It became a sort of annex to the park, with its numerous open-air cafés and restaurants, one of which still exists today: the prestigious Villa Lorraine, which was a café, restaurant and boarding house when it was founded by restaurateur Trippa-Dekoster in 1893.

NEARBY
Anachronistic architectural grouping ②
Chaussée de Waterloo 878–880

This group of buildings along chaussée de Waterloo represents a disconcerting use of anachronism. Built from 1934 to 1938, this grouping by architect Léon Smets blends a variety of historic styles, such as Baroque or Louis XV. The architect was even so refined as to use materials that perfectly imitate the original architecture. A large archway extending from the right side of the main façade leads to the garden. To the left there is a wrought-iron shop sign featuring a cherub, and to the right a Baroque-inspired fountain topped with a high-relief based on a work by Michelangelo.

RIDING SHELTERS IN THE BOIS DE LA CAMBRE

To keep feet and hooves dry

Bois de la Cambre
Allée des Amazones and chemin de l'Aube

The Bois de la Cambre is a popular spot for horse riding and was originally home to three shelters built by landscape architect Edouard Keilig (1827-1895) to protect riders and their horses in the event of storms and heavy rain.

They are all three different shapes: the first is hexagonal (built in 1872), the second octagonal (dating from 1878 – this is the largest) and the last round (built in 1882 – a mushroom-shaped shelter, also known as a parasol shelter).

While the hexagonal shelter on chemin des Anémones has now disappeared (vandalised in 2015), the octagonal shelter on chemin de l'Aube and the mushroom-shaped shelter (the most remarkable – see photo) on allée des Amazones are still clearly visible.

Their height offers the opportunity to admire their surprising framework and to notice that their central and main support is none other than the trunk of a beautiful tree.

The Bois de la Cambre was designed from scratch in 1862 by Edouard Keilig, a landscape architect of German origin. Designed in the 'English style', the park was a social gathering place for the people of Brussels, who strolled around in buggies, horse-drawn carriages and prams. This wooded, bucolic and hilly area offered beautiful views and was home to a velodrome, a racecourse, a gymnasium, the Théâtre de Poche, a dairy (now a restaurant) and a few wooden houses, such as the Robinson chalet on its island in the middle of the lake, rebuilt after a fire and still very popular with Brussels residents.

A game of cricket in 1815

In 1815, on the eve of the Battle of Waterloo, the English played cricket in what is now the Bois de la Cambre. This part of the woods is known as the 'Pelouse des Anglais' (English Green), and since 1965 a memorial stele and an oak tree commemorate this moment in sporting history.

NEARBY

Horseshoe-shaped pedestrian crossings

The allée du Turf that connects the Bois de la Cambre to the Forêt de Soignes is normally reserved for horse riders. It also crosses other roads (namely the Drève Saint-Hubert), which explains the very pleasant horseshoe-shaped crossings.

© GdML

CARRÉ TILLENS

1.5 hectares of vegetable plots cultivated by local residents

Rue du Fossé between Chaussée d'Alsemberg 561 and 565
Rue Joseph Bens 9–11
Rue Roosendael 192
Tram No. 51, Bens stop

C arré Tillens, practically invisible from the street, is a marvellous place.

Occupying an entire block, it consists of 1.5 hectares of vegetable plots open to the public: the paths across the area, unlike most of the Brussels allotments, are also through routes from one street to another and are completely accessible.

The easiest way to get in is by rue Roosendael. Coming from chaussée d'Alsemberg, go past several buildings before you reach an eye-catching fence.

On tiptoe, try to get a look at the greenery in what appears to be a large garden. Don't waste your energy trying a little door that won't open, but carry on a little further until you come across a narrow path that winds lazily down to the left, opposite 192 rue de Roosendael.

And there it is. After a short distance a feeling of well-satisfied curiosity fills you. A kindly-looking woman is busily digging her plot, three local retired people quietly chatting are delighted to help you.

There are 44 plots here, offered for rent by the Institut Bruxellois de la Gestion de l'Environnement (IBGE).

Although in theory anyone can rent some land, in practice the plots are reserved for local residents to ensure that the gardens are well maintained.

Carry on down the path and you'll meet a couple embracing on a patch of lawn.

Further still, a woman brings along some of her kitchen rubbish (orange peel, wilted salad leaves, etc.) and adds it to a large container to rot down into compost, which will later be used as fertilizer. Just like in the country.

NEARBY

Square Coghen ⑤

An attractive housing estate which, on very sloping ground, offers fine inter-war houses. Look out particularly for No. 42 to 46 (architect Pierre Verbruggen) and 9 and 11 (Josse Franssen), as well as those from 75 to 87 (Louis Herman De Koninck).

Carré Stevens
Chaussée d'Alsemberg, between 461 and 463

Carré Pauwels ⑦
Chaussée d'Alsemberg between 469 and 471

Not far from the marvellous carré Tillens, carrés Stevens and Pauwels form two charming impasses communicating with each other. On each side, houses with gardens give the impression of being in a small village, far from the exhaust fumes of chaussée d'Alsemberg.

Carrés Sersté, Cassimans and Meert ⑧
Carré Cassimans, Rue de Boetendael between 132 and 140; carré Sersté on the left of Rue des Carmélites 126 and at Rue de Boetendael 96

Although the carré Meert is now private and inaccessible, it offers attractive vantage points for walkers and a particularly agreeable lifestyle for residents.

Uccle 'squares'

Uccle is the only district in Brussels to have successfully preserved most of its old rural impasses (dead ends). It's surprising but true that most of these impasses, known also as 'squares' (*'karrei'* in Flemish popular parlance and *'blok'* in Dutch), aren't square at all. The origin of this designation goes back to the 18th century. At that time, there were no street signs giving the official place names. Usage prevailed and the current designation is thus the result of popular tradition and the habits of local residents.

Such was the case of 35–39 rue aux Choux, which had a large square courtyard behind the houses, giving onto the road. Set back from the public highway, it was known locally as the *bataillon carré* (parade ground).

It kept this name a long time, even after the local authorities officially designated it Saint-Félix in 1853. The name *bataillon carré* became rather fashionable and was gradually taken up by other residents who used it to name other similar impasses, generally square in shape.

Over time, the square part of the name came to dominate and served quite simply to describe even long and narrow alleys.

In 1853, a directive from the city of Brussels launched a general revision of public street names and enforced the word impasse to replace the various *culs-de-sac, trous, portes, allées, cours, coins* and *carrés*. The Brussels suburbs didn't apply this legislation and Uccle was able to keep its attractive *carrés*.

CHEMIN DU CRABBEGAT

⑨

One of the prettiest paths in Brussels

Avenue de Fré, avenue Kamerdelle
Bus No. 38, 41, 43 or 98, Héros stop

T his relatively wide, cobbled path is perhaps one of the prettiest in Brussels, even though it is better known than the nearby Delleweg. It opens out quite widely at the corner of the Vieux Cornet, avenue de Fré, where there is a restaurant.

Take this track which leads up into the forest. After a few minutes the track forks. Straight ahead, it leads to an overhead bridge. A favourite subject of many Uccle artists, the bridge is now in poor repair and the original route is barred. To carry on beyond the bridge, climb up the slope on the right to go round the bridge and eventually you'll arrive at avenue Paul Stroobant.

The section after the bridge is less pleasant. Rather choose the left fork, which takes you after a few minutes to avenue Kamerdelle. Still just as agreeable, it passes various private properties as well as a tennis club on the right. At the sides of the road a few dilapidated lamp standards await restoration.

The tennis club, which can be reached directly from the road, has a very nice terrace where you can have a drink or snack. From the terrace the view is extremely restful, both of the beaten-earth courts and the surrounding trees. No city noise filters out here.

The Crabbegat site was listed in 1989.

NEARBY
Studio of Paul-Auguste Masui ⑩
Chemin du Crabbegat 4a
02 374 63 12

If you phone beforehand, you can visit the former studio of Paul-Auguste Masui in a reconstruction using 18th-century Flemish building materials. There, from 1928 until the 1980s, far from the crowded streets, Masui created engravings in wood and copper, etchings, lithographs, pastel drawings, gouache, watercolours, oil paintings and sculptures.

Run by the Fondation Isabelle Masui, the site includes the artist's former home and some 17th-century stables. It can be hired for cultural events.

CHEMIN DU DELLEWEG

Are we really in Brussels?

Right of No. 118 in rue Victor Allard
Tram No. 48, Victor Allard stop

Missing from most Brussels maps, the chemin du Delleweg is a remarkable surprise, a short distance from Uccle's Maison Communale (community centre). Hidden between the house at 118 rue Victor Allard and a clump of trees, the entry is scarcely visible and very narrow. Push your way through into the small passage. After a few steps the path widens and you come across the enchanting and surprising vista of a wooded path, tranquilly twisting down a valley. A few wooden steps quickly lead you down, to a strong feeling of having discovered a little secret passage.

Two or three minutes are all it takes to rejoin the other side of the track which comes out on avenue de la Princesse Paola, among some up-market houses.

Listed in 1998, Delleweg (on the left going down) runs alongside the large property known as Domaine d'Allard, after a wealthy banking family whose most illustrious member, Victor Allard, was bourgmestre of Uccle from 1895 to 1899. The house, built shortly before 1900, is in the Flemish neo-Renaissance style. You can only glimpse it by returning via avenue Victor Gambier where the formal entrance to the property is to be found at No. 57.

Just opposite the entrance, look out for a picturesque group of small 19th-century houses, typical of popular dwellings of the time with their communal alley at the rear and small private gardens set within, visible from the corner of rue Labarre.

NEARBY
Chemin du Vossegat (12)
Rue Beeckman between 127 and 129 and linking rue Beeckman to rue Auguste Danse
Chemin du Vossegat is a pleasant paved walkway, just as surprising to find in such an urban setting.

Carré Peeters
Rue de Stalle between No. 92 and 94
An attractive impasse bordered with little houses with private gardens. It recalls the industrial past of rue de Stalle, where there were many workers' houses of this type before the street was turned over to the service sector.

SITE OF NECKERSGAT –
THE WATER MILL

One of the last former pulp mills

Rue Keyenbempt 66
Tram No. 82, Keyenbempt stop

The Neckersgat site was already occupied in the Neolithic Period (6000 BC) and probably at the time of the Celts, as archaeological digs have shown. Still verdant today, it offers the curious walker a lovely route to discover the Neckersgat mill.

The most romantic route is via the Institut National des Invalides at 36 avenue Achille Reisdorff. Constructed in 1844 by the landowner, Jean-Baptiste Gaucheret, the building was turned into a chateau by his descendant Marie-Thérèse de Gaucheret. It was then converted into a clinic, a military hospital and a sanatorium before being acquired in 1927 by the Institute, which still uses it as a rest-home for war victims.

If you ask nicely, the employees will probably guide you to the start of the path that leads to the mill. The track winding down the hill from the Institute offers a pleasantly picturesque view of the valley below. As you head down the track the forest grows denser and the town is completely forgotten. Stay on the track as it runs alongside a small pond, and after five minutes you'll reach the back of the mill. A little gate only has to be opened to let you rejoin rue Keyenbempt and the front entrance to the mill.

© Tram Bruxelles

Neckersgat mill, originally simply for grain, is along with the Crockaert mill on rue de Lindebeek, also in Uccle, the last example of pulp mills for paper-making.

Installed at cours du Geleytsbeek where a mill-wheel, now gone, was operated, the mill was converted into living accommodation and ceased all industrial activity. Acquired by the district of Uccle in 1970, the mill was listed in 1971 and the site in 1977.

Several little tracks, the ordinary, less picturesque access routes, lead away to the left of the mill. You can, on the other hand, continue your walk on the opposite side: keeping to the left of the road as soon as it reappears, you'll make your forest walk last a little longer before finally emerging at the start of chaussée de St-Job.

NEARBY
Gregoire House Observatory ⑮
Dieweg 292
02 372 05 38 – bnprojects.be

Built in 1933 by Henry van de Velde, the Grégoire house is a beautiful modern residence. It is however possible to visit it during the exhibitions organized by the Observatoire Galerie which, since 1995, has presented young international artists. The dual function of the house gives a special appeal to the visit. In discovering the various works of art, you have an overwhelming feeling of being in the home of a private collector: wandering around, you soak up the atmosphere with some surprise at having landed among this particularly refined lifestyle.

CHEMIN AVIJL

Don't wait too long to visit: housing projects are in full swing

Chaussée de Saint-Job 701
Bus No. 43, De Wansijn stop

Chemin Avijl is one of those country roads in the north of Uccle among the most rural in the district. It begins (according to certain plans) to the left of 70 chaussée St-Job, runs to rue Jean Benaets and carries on to the left a short distance before reaching a point just below the summit of the plateau. The view is amazing: straight in front of you, the road plays out, fringed to the left by pretty houses. To the right is the countryside, one vegetable plot after another, among rampant grass and trees.

If you follow the path on the plateau that runs parallel to chemin Avijl in the opposite direction, keeping to the right, after a few minutes you'll come back to rue Jean Benaets, by a school that you would have passed earlier. If you follow this same path but pushing along in the opposite direction from which you came, and keeping to the left, the countryside becomes more omnipresent, the forest comes into view and you're all set for a long walk. Coming back to the road itself, keep straight on to reach Vieille Rue du Moulin.

Don't wait too long to see these few special places, as property developers have been at the ready for a while and housing projects are in full swing.

Just nearby, there is a pretty impasse at No. 66–80 rue de la Montagne de St-Job and at No. 90 a lovely passage that comes out at No. 51 rue du Ham.

NEARBY
The observatory's inclining lamps ⑰
Avenue Circulaire

The lamp standards on the columns framing the main gate of the Observatory are remarkable for a one thing in particular: their light is directed by side-panels so as not to interfere with the nocturnal activities nearby.

Unfortunately these are the last examples of this superb urban detail: before, all the lamps on avenue Circulaire respected the astronomers by avoiding all light pollution. Those lamps were even more refined in that they were steeply curved towards the ground, like swans' necks. They were, sadly, replaced by the local authorities a few years ago. A little of the city magic gone…

It was probably one of these lamps that Tintin's dog Milou ('Snowy' in translation) bumped into in the early pages of *L'Étoile Mystérieuse* (The Shooting Star), which is set partly in and around the Observatory.

FOREST WARDEN MONUMENT

A menhir for every forest warden

Chemin du Grasdelle, near the junction of drève du Haras and avenue Alfred Dubois
Car park at the first hump on avenue Alfred Dubois when coming from the Drève de Lorraine

The beautiful valley of Grasdelle lies at the fringes of the Uccle and Rhode-Saint-Genèse districts. This small valley, which is mowed regularly to preserve the vegetation that is typical of such open meadows, conceals a war memorial imbued with spirituality and contemplation that is far from the typical patriotic fanfares. This homage to eleven forest wardens killed in action during the First World War is composed of eleven large stones erected, like menhirs, around a megalithic gate reminiscent of a dolmen.

Each menhir perpetuates the name of one of the wardens. This monument was erected in 1920 by Brabant sculptor Richard Viandier (1858–1949). He used a rather strange stone called the pudding stone of Wéris, a concrete-like conglomerate of pebbles held together by a kind of natural cement.

Forêt de Soignes

For centuries, the Sonian Forest has been the place to enjoy the quintessential sport of princes: hunting. As the country suffered occupation after occupation, the forest passed from hand to hand, belonging successively to the dukes of Brabant, the dukes of Burgundy, the Hapsburgs, the French Government and William I, Prince of Orange. It then passed into the darkest period of its history when it fell into the hands of the Société Générale pour Favoriser l'Industrie Nationale (General Society to Encourage National Industries), which cleared some 7,000 hectares of the forest between 1831 and 1843. The forest was finally returned to the Belgian Government in 1843. Originally of English oaks, it became a forest of beech trees planted in the 18th century during the Austrian period, which explains why it is still largely a cathedral forest today. The forest covers land in three national regions: 1,620 hectares, or 38 per cent of its total surface area and almost one-tenth of the region's territory, lies in the Brussels-Capital region, 56 per cent lies in Flanders and 6 per cent in Wallonia.

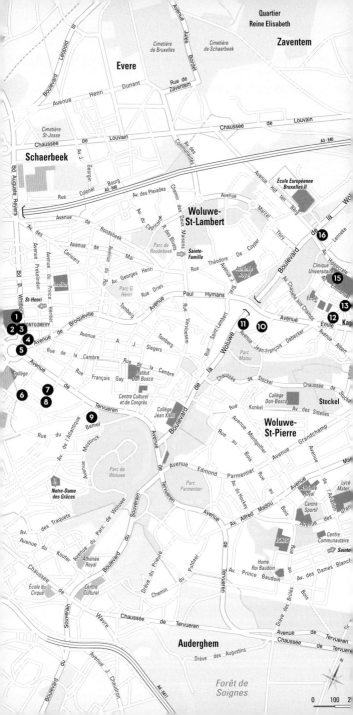

Woluwe-Saint-Pierre, Woluwe-Saint-Lambert

CASTEL DE LINTHOUT

Dive into the neo-Gothic period

Avenue des Deux Tilleuls 2
Admission sometimes possible if you ask nicely
Metro or tram No. 23, 24, 25, 39, 44 and 80, Montgomery stop

Within the grounds of the Institut du Sacré-Cœur of Lindthout, the aptly named '*Castel*' (mansion), was formerly a private residence. The house, built from 1867 to 1869 by Ghent architect Florimond Vandepoele, was given its current form by architect Edmond De Vigne in 1898 for his client, the captain of industry Charles-Henri Dietrich, as related by the inscription on the front façade. Dietrich didn't live in the house very long, preferring the well-known Val Duchesse priory. In 1903, he transferred the estate to the nuns of Lille's Sacred Heart Church. It later fell into disuse and was eventually bought by the village of Woluwe-Saint-Lambert in 2000, which turned it into a school of music, dance and the performing arts.

Now magnificently restored, this mysterious edifice has preserved all of its neo-Gothic interior. The site is not officially open to visitors, but if you ask politely, you'll probably be allowed a quick glance inside.

From the moment you enter the foyer, the Gothic architecture sets the tone. It is enhanced by paintings depicting landmarks of the Woluwe-Saint-Lambert of yesteryear: the old village, the Lindekemale mill, the Hof ten Berg (an old farm belonging to Abbaye de Forest), and a pond. The corridor on the right leads to the mansion's star attraction: the ballroom, which the nuns (quite understandably) used as a chapel and which today is the perfect venue for concerts and school rehearsals.

Lit by a rose window, the room is topped by a wooden ceiling in the shape of a boat's hull. Other rooms are similarly decorated, such as the main staircase or the rooms on the first floor (the 'ceramics room', the 'Renaissance room' or the 'golden sitting room'), but none of them matches the magic of the ballroom.

NEARBY
Ceramic panels ②
Avenue Henri Dietrich 27

On the house at avenue Dietrich 27, two large ceramic panels depict women picking flowers. Produced by the Helman factory of Berchem-Sainte-Agathe, and probably based on a drawing by Jacques Madiol, they have been wonderfully preserved. This house designed by architect A. Aulbur in 1906 also has a magnificent wrought-iron and glass awning.

THE HOUSE AT AVENUE DE TERVUEREN 120

The death and resurrection of a house

Metro or trams No. 23, 24, 25, 39, 44 and 80, Montgomery stop

© Jean-Jacques Evrard

The house at No. 120 avenue de Tervueren was once so widely talked about that it has recently become the symbol of advocates for cultural preservation.

It all started on 23 October 1991, when the village of Woluwe-Saint-Pierre granted a demolition permit for this mansion designed in a geometric Art Nouveau style in 1906 by architect Paul Hamesse. The plan was to replace it with a building of stores, offices and apartments designed by architect Marc Corbiau, a plan that aroused public indignation. Petitions were signed and, finally, on 26 March 1992, a stop order for reasons of historic preservation (the façade and roof) was issued, but too late: the building was hastily demolished.

On the evening of 21 May 1993, a crane pushed the façade over onto a bed of sand. Elements of the façade, particularly those in blue stone, were recuperated to be used again. Damaged during the demolition, they had to be restored and were stocked in a village warehouse. Today, the house has been rebuilt and has rediscovered its former prestige, on the outside at least.

NEARBY
ICHEC ④
Boulevard Brand Whitlock 2

In the 1910s, many aristocrats took up residence on boulevard Brand Whitlock and had their mansions built, each one more magnificent than the next. But customs change with the times. In 1962, No. 2, at the corner of Montgomery Square, was renovated to house the offices and classrooms of the Institut Catholique des Hautes Etudes Commerciales (ICHEC).

The foyer and staircase are accessible during the institute's teaching hours. It is sometimes possible to take a discreet look. The original decor has been preserved, illustrating the past splendour of this mansion designed by the architect Dufas in 1912. The stone staircase is lit by stained-glass windows and its landings are decorated with a splendid mosaic of marble that is a true pleasure to the eye.

THE HIGHCHAIR
OF MONTGOMERY SQUARE

A bit of height, by Jove!

Artwork by Peter Weidenbaum and poem by Agnieszka Kuciak
Square Montgomery, near boulevard Saint-Michel
versbruxelles.be
Metro or trams No. 23, 24, 25, 39, 44 and 80, Montgomery stop

This sculpture seems so out of place on Montgomery Square that many people don't even notice it. Directly in line with boulevard Saint-Michel as you look towards Montgomery Square, a thin, 4 m high stainless-steel chair looks out over the entire neighbourhood, providing a welcome change from the hectic traffic and general hustle and bustle of the Eurocrats, students and diplomats. At the foot of this surrealist perch, a poem describes the site and adds some much-needed soul to the square.

This installation, erected in June, 2008, is the result of a period of reflection on the neighbourhood carried out by poetess Agnieszka Kuciak and visual artist Peter Weidenbaum. The Brussels literary association Het Beschrijf brought these two artists together as part of the 'Vers Bruxelles' project, whose purpose was to bring a modicum of poetry to everyday life. Since 2008, twelve such poetic works resulting from the collaboration of poets and visual artists have come to life throughout the city, from the city centre to Molenbeek, Anderlecht and Forest.

NEARBY

Houses designed by architect Jean De Ligne ⑥
Rue Maurice Liétard 30–32, 34, 44, 52, 56–58, 62 and 64
The neighbourhood around Saint-Michel secondary school conceals several little architectural treasures. From 1912 to 1923, architect Jean De Ligne designed seven houses on rue Maurice Liétard. Although they seem simple at first look, these façades foreshadow the strict geometry of the Art Deco style and offer interesting details, such as stained-glass windows, in a style influenced by the Dutch architecture (bricks, wooden shutters) that was so popular at the time.

House and studio of Émile Fabry ⑦
Rue du Collège Saint-Michel 6
Symbolist painter Émile Fabry once lived at No. 6 rue du Collège Saint-Michel. Designed by architect Émile Lamblot in 1902, the originality of this simple home lies in the large glass roof over the studio and a small door that let the artist remove his monumental paintings. On either side of the door, terracotta reliefs catch the eye.

Philippe and Marcel Wolfers Studio ⑧
Avenue Roger Vandendriessche 28A
A beautiful wrought-iron fence representing vines, a common Art Nouveau motif, marks the location of the former workshop of Philippe Wolfers, a famous Brussels sculptor and silversmith, and of his son Marcel, who was also a sculptor. The house was designed by architect Émile Van Nooten in 1906.

Books and rattles

Rue du Bemel 23
02 770 53 33
wittockiana.org
Tuesday to Saturday, 10am–5pm; closed public holidays
Trams No. 39 or 44, Chien vert stop

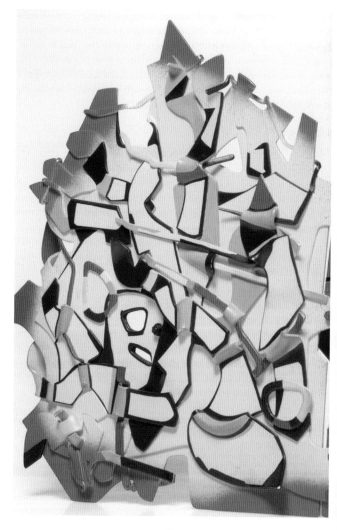

Here, you'll find one of the largest collections of precious books and bindings in the world. Michel Wittock bought his first book from a secondhand bookseller on rue de la Madeleine at the age of 14 and caught a serious case of the collector's bug. Today, at over 70 years old, this former manufacturer is the owner of one of the most beautiful collections of precious books and bindings in the world. In 1981, Michel Wittock inaugurated the Bibliotheca Wittockiana, a museum to house and display his fabulous finds.

Originally limited to one floor and only open to a few friends and lucky guests, the small museum designed by architect Emmanuel de Callataÿ grew over time and is now open to the public.

In 1995, a second phase of construction began, led by the same architect, Callataÿ, and Michel's own son, architect Charly Wittock. The result is a particularly interesting building whose rather opaque ground floor made from rough concrete and blue stone contrasts with the large windows of the upper floor, which houses the library that is thus visible from the street. Over time, Mr Wittock's collectionitis took on a new dimension.

What began as an exciting and scholarly search for ancient works has turned into the calmer approach of a patron of the arts, which has encouraged him to order bindings by contemporary artists. The Wittockiana holds over 5,000 precious works, ranging from bindings and manuscripts to autographs and books by artists, which are shown to the public during exhibitions organized by the staff, under the leadership of Michel Wittock himself.

The staff is very active, as they put on three or four exhibitions every year that are often related to Brussels' cultural calendar (consult the website for information about the current exhibition).

An unusual collection of rattles

The library also holds an unusual and original collection of rattles. Considered to be the oldest toy in the world, these baby toys have continued to evolve through the ages according to technological advances and levels of society.

Five hundred rattles, some of which date back to 2000 BC, are preserved here. A selection is on permanent display at the back of the museum.

CHAPEL OF MARIE-LA-MISÉRABLE

Mary's misfortunes

Avenue de la Chapelle
02 770 30 87
Daily, 7.30am–6pm
Metro Vandervelde

Just a few metres from avenue Émile Vandervelde, time stands still. The modest and forgotten Chapel of the Blessed Mary the Miserable is undoubtedly the most touching sanctuary in Brussels. Built in the 14th century, it is recognizable by the little turret that rises at the centre of the roof.

The back of the chapel is connected to the former chaplain's home, whose slender, Gothic lines rival those of the old trees that border it. A garden designed by landscaper René Péchère in 1975 surrounds the chapel.

Don't hesitate to step through the door of this old sanctuary. The simple, sombre and straight nave is still bordered by a continuous stone bench and is separated from the choir by an oak screen. In the choir, the centre of an altarpiece dating from 1609 depicts the Virgin of the Seven Sorrows while the side panels illustrate the story of Mary the Miserable, like a strip cartoon. Mary the Miserable desired only one thing: to pray and live on charity. But one day, a rich young man wanted to seduce her. Rejected, he sought his revenge by placing a valuable object in the young girl's pouch. He accused her of theft and she was condemned to be buried alive. This little church was later built on the site of her martyrdom.

A small side chapel conceals a curious, oblong oak object – a collection box dating from 1574 that held the offerings of pilgrims who, over the centuries, came to pray near the young woman's relics.

NEARBY
Lindekemale Mill and chemin du Vellemolen ⑪
Avenue Jean-François Debecker 6

Set in motion by the waters of the Woluwe river, the Lindekemale Mill, the origins of which date back to the 12th century, is one of the oldest in the Brussels area. For centuries, it was used to mill grain before becoming a paper mill in the 19th century. A historic monument since 1989, it stands modestly across from the impudent Woluwe Shopping Centre: two images of the city are thus confronted here. On the other side of rue Jean-François Debecker, an old path follows the Woluwe and joins up with avenue Émile Vandervelde. The water, which is particularly pure here, is bordered by luxurious, indigenous vegetation.

CITÉ-JARDIN DU KAPELLEVELD ⑫

Different styles in harmony

Either side of avenue Émile Vandervelde: avenues de l'Idéal, du Rêve, du Bois Jean, de la Semois, de la Lesse, de la Claireau, Albert Dumont and Marcel Devienne
Metro Vandervelde

Garden cities can often be found on the fringes of the villages that make up the second ring of Brussels' suburbs, and this is no exception. Located on the edge of the Louvain-en-Woluwe campus and the border of Crainhem, the Keppelleveld estate was designed by town planner and landscaper Louis Van der Swaelmen, who also drew up the plans for the famous garden cities of Logis and Floréal at Watermael-Boitsfort (which you must visit if you haven't already). Here, the houses are spread along the simple lines of streets that lie perpendicular to avenue Vandervelde, which passes through the site and existed before the garden city. From 1922 to 1926, 449 houses based on

© EmDee

19 different types were designed by four avant-garde architects: Huib Hoste, Antoine Pompe, Jean-François Hoeben and Paul Rubbers. The different styles corresponded to the architectural tastes of each of these architects. So, from one street to another, the ambiance changes from a more modern style, with lines of abstract and level façades beneath flat roofs, to a more 'Flemish Beguine convent' type of style, with houses topped with large tiled roofs.

Despite these differences of design, there is a great feeling of coherence thanks to the attention Louis Van der Swaelment paid to the clever layout and size of the grassed areas, as each house has a small patch of garden in front of it and a large garden at the back. The Kapelleveld estate, which is still owned by the cooperative that financed the project, has been very well preserved. Unfortunately, however, the original wooden window frames have been replaced with PVC frames. Since its conception, a genuine sense of unity has reigned over this estate and, in 1934, it materialized in the Kapelleveld Civic Centre, whose main concern is the physical and intellectual well-being of the residents.

© EmDee

PAUL MOENS MEDICINAL PLANT GARDEN

The courtyard of miracles

Between avenue Emmanuel Mounier and avenue de l'Idéal
Free admission to the park from 1 April to 31 October, 9am–6pm
02 764 41 28 or info-jardins@uclouvain.be
Guided tours by reservation at 2pm on the last Sunday of the month or by request
Duration: about 2 hours
Metro Alma or Crainhem

In the tradition of medieval medicinal gardens, the University of Louvain-en-Woluwe possesses a marvellous half-acre enclosure in the centre of a sculpture garden. Here, 400 medicinal, condiment, edible and toxic plants, both land and aquatic, are gathered here on as many plots of land.

This enclosed garden, which opened in 1975, was the fruit of the enthusiastic hard work of Professor Paul Moens and his team of volunteers. A small plaque supplies the name of each plant in Latin and its common name in French.

The colour of the plaque indicates the plant's toxicity: white if the plant is considered non-toxic in normal doses, yellow when it contains some toxic substances, and red (there are a few) when the plant is deadly or dangerous to handle. Although most of the plants are easily recognizable, we are often unfamiliar with their virtues. The properties of each plant are described with one or more adjectives, which neophytes sometimes find difficult to understand.

Here are a few terms to start with: an anthelmintic provokes the elimination of intestinal worms; an astringent tightens living tissue; a carminative helps release intestinal gases; a cholagogic helps drain bile; a choleretic stimulates biliary secretions; a haemostatic stops haemorrhaging; a stomachic helps digestion; and a vulnerary heals wounds.

NEARBY
Monastery of the Visitation (14)
Avenue d'Hébron 5 (Kraainem)

From avenue Hippocrate, near the entrance to the car park of the same name and opposite the Descente de la Dunette, a hidden path leads secretly to Flanders. On the border between Crainhem, Zaventem and Woluwe, an Art Deco style convent, built in the late 1920s by the monk and architect Dom Bellot, marvellously illustrates all the architectural potential of brick. It is still occupied by the Visitandines, a religious order whose members live cloistered. Only the chapel is open to the public for Sunday morning Mass. The chapel's L shape hides the nuns' stalls from the eyes of the public.

UCL CAMPUS

15

A utopian campus

Woluwe-Saint-Lambert
Metro Alma

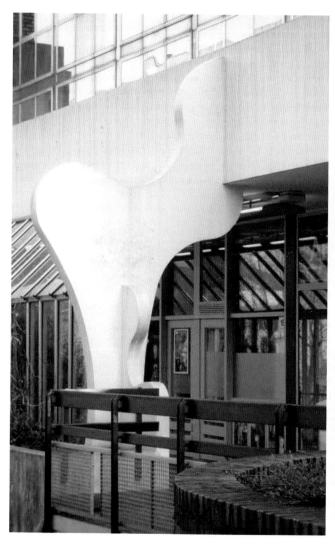

Many Brussels residents are curiously unaware that, 40 years ago, Louvain-en-Woluwe was the site of an extraordinary architectural and human experience. As a result of the events of May 1968 and the 'Walen buiten' crisis, which resulted in the split of the University of Louvain, the UCL decided to set up the medical school at Woluwe-Saint-Lambert, next to the site of Louvain-La-Neuve. For most of the student buildings (residence halls, university cafeterias and shops as well as administrative offices, metro station, day-care and primary school), the academic authorities turned to the wonderfully turbulent architect, Lucien Kroll, a decision that was approved by the students. The central idea of the project was to initiate the creative participation of future residents to 'build a lifestyle rather than a set of detailed plans.'

Far from the cold atmosphere of standardized buildings, the centre of the Louvain-en-Woluwe campus bears the stamp of this imaginative beginning. Although the project wasn't fully completed (of the original 40,000 m², the Kroll agency only finished half due to a divergence of opinion with UCL), the revolutionary intelligence of the project – its playful and designedly childish aspect – is clearly visible in this happy disorder that would have pleased even Antoni Gaudí. To fully appreciate the extent of this project, take the metro as far as the Alma stop.

Here, you won't find works of art that were just added to brighten up the place, because the station is a work of art in itself. Its concrete posts resemble a colourful and textured forest, while its pavement-like platform serves as a sort of peristyle leading to the campus. Across from the station, buildings rise and fall, miraculously escaping any form of rationality in a quasi-medieval entanglement of frames, boards and sheets of Eternit sticking out of all sorts of terraces.

One building is called 'Mémé' (short for Maison Médicale, or medical building), while the other is pretentiously called 'Mairie' (meaning the town hall). Their chaotic exterior, which resembles a shanty town as much as it does an abstract painting, reflects the maze inside. The common boundaries between the outside and the inside are blurred by openings of all sorts. As they aren't always fixed in place, the location of these openings can be moved in relation to the changing uses of the space, thanks to moveable and collapsible partitions.

THE WORK OF
THE HOF TER MUSSCHEN

16

Participate in the preservation of the Brabant countryside

First Saturday of the month, 10am–4.30pm, at the corner of avenue Hippocrate and boulevard de la Woluwe
cebe.be
Metro Alma or bus No. 42 or 79, Hof ter Musschen stop

For nearly two decades now, the Hof ter Musschen site has been taken over and managed by a group of enthusiasts united to form the Commission de l'Environnement de Bruxelles et Environs (CEBE, Environmental Commission of Brussels and Surrounding Area), one of the main goals of which is to maintain biological diversity in Brussels.

The Sparrows Farm, which you can see from boulevard de la Woluwe which passes below, is a relic of Brabant's rural countryside. Delightfully and surrealistically located in the middle of the city, it spreads over several hectares along the lower eastern side of the Woluwe river. The site is dotted with various buildings that have a rich cultural heritage, some of which are listed as historic buildings and most of which are not managed by the CEBE. Among them are a beautiful, square-shaped farm that operated until 1979 (the oldest sections date back to the 15th century and have

unfortunately been overly restored), a mill that has been demolished and rebuilt numerous times, and a hayloft with a bread oven. Notable for its old buildings, the site is also remarkable for its varied landscape: prairies, wet prairies, orchards, woods and sunken lanes.

On the first Saturday of the month, throughout the year, the CEBE invites people of all ages to take part in preserving this site. The preservation work, which follows an ecological management plan, is essential, as it protects the diversity of the site's fauna and flora. Indeed, it helps keep these diverse and unique landscapes from turning back into simple wooded areas.

So, in the summer, the prairies are mowed. Volunteers whose minds are filled with images of yesteryear (generally the first-time volunteers) may choose to use a scythe, while the more realistic volunteers prefer to use edge trimmers. In autumn and winter, the workers cut down some trees and prune others, they trim the quickset hedges and pollard the willow trees. The number of volunteers varies from four or five to more than a dozen, but all of them participate in this extraordinary and useful experience.

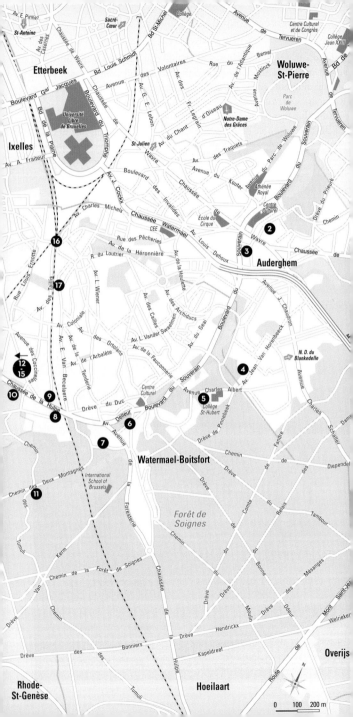

Auderghem
Watermael-Boitsfort

CHÂTEAU
DE TROIS FONTAINES

Two castles lost in the forest

Château de Trois-Fontaines
Chaussée de Wavre 2241
Château de la Solitude
Avenue Charles Schaller 54
Bus No. 72, ADEPS stop

T he Château de Trois-Fontaines, or at least what is left of it, is located at the end of chaussée de Wavre, below the highway viaduct near the Léonard intersection.

On the left, a pond at the end of the valley curiously appears larger next to this old residence of white rubble stone, brick and cross-bar windows. Left abandoned during the French occupation, the château fell into ruin. Today, only the central section of the main residence remains. It dates back to the 16th century and, inside, there is an old Gothic fireplace and a stone bench recessed in the wall.

It was in this dark, wet corner of the world that brigands, thieves and poachers were imprisoned in the 16th century. From time to time, it was also used to house master rabbit warrens (a type of gamekeeper) or forest wardens (in fact, the Brussels-Environment organization still manages the estate). By taking the chemin des Trois Couleurs above the Château de Trois-Fontaines, and then turning right on the chemin de Blankedelle, you end up on avenue Charles Schaller, where, at No. 54, you'll find the imposing Château de Solitude standing at the edge of the forest.

This castle was erected in 1912 for Her Serene Highness, Princess Marie-Ludmilla of Arenberg. Here, the disconsolate widow of Duke Charles-Albert de Croÿ devoted herself to protecting the animals she sheltered on her sumptuous yet solitary estate. She even had a cemetery laid out especially for them.

Designed in Beaux-Arts style by architect François Malfait, the château, with its white façades and strict symmetry, brings the Louis XVI style up to date. Now the headquarters of the International University Sports Federation, the château was remarkably restored after years of neglect. Although it isn't generally open to visitors, you can try to catch a glimpse of the foyer by making a polite request during office hours.

RUES DE LA PENTE
AND DU VERGER

Play hide-and-seek with the old village

Metro Hermann-Debroux or bus No. 34, Bergoje stop

Auderghem has a modest rural past that, although rather well hidden, is revealed from time to time. Near chaussée de Wavre, in two tiny *strootjes* located between rue des Villageois on one side and rue du Vieux Moulin on the other, you'll find rue de la Pente and rue du Verger. These two former thoroughfares, which are now narrow, pedestrian, and badly paved, seem out of place, but they are witnesses of the Auderghem of yesteryear.

Rue de la Pente is the smallest and more picturesque of the two, since the homes on rue du Verger date from a slightly later period, with some dating from the 1920s. From the 18th century to the beginning of the 20th century, the village of Auderghem covered these streets and the entire hillside.

Once called Loozenberg (Lice Hill), this hillside's unflattering name was changed a century ago to Bergoje, a local version of the Flemish word *Berghuizen* (Houses on the Hill). Indeed, this hill, crossed by chausée de Wavre, was dotted with the small homes of workers and day labourers; most of those still standing today date from the late 19th century. On both sides of chaussée de Wavre, between No. 1800 and 1900, are *cul-de-sacs* lined with the same type of houses.

NEARBY
Parc du Bergoje ③
Rue Jacques Bassem, opposite Rue Paul Vereyleweghen
This small park bordered by office buildings was developed in 1994 by the Brussels Environment organization and was once part of the Sonian Forest. A little stream runs through it, the Roodkloosterbeek, which as its name indicates leads to Rouge-Cloître (Red Cloister) after crossing chaussée de Wavre.

Private home of architect Henri Lacoste ④
Avenue Jean Van Horenbeeck 147
Although largely unknown, Henri Lacoste (1885–1968) was nevertheless a major Belgian architect. Also a professor, archaeologist and creator, he essentially worked during the interwar period, imparting the Art Deco style with his imagination nourished by exoticism, dream and refinement. His private home, which dates from 1926, bears witness to his art (don't hesitate to take a look at the left side of the house). Although they appear rather simple at first glance, the façades are filled with a myriad of details that blend elements of Greek, Assyrian, medieval, Renaissance and Art Deco architecture. A final, almost childish, touch is the large grasshopper that decorates the arch of the door.

CHÂTEAU CHARLE-ALBERT

An old haunted château completely restored to its former condition

Avenue Charle-Albert 5–7
Visible from outside
Closed to visitors
Tram No. 94 and bus No. 95, Wiener stop

© Jean-Jacques Evrard

Château Charle-Albert ranks as one of the completely unknown jewels of the architectural heritage of Brussels. At this particular point, avenue Charle-Albert is a one-way avenue, isolated, and frequented almost exclusively by the employees of the insurance company whose offices are located opposite.

An artist and interior designer who made his fortune from the high-ranking nobility and bourgeoisie in Belgium and abroad during the second half of the 19th century, Albert Charles (known commonly as Charles-Albert, thus giving the château its name) designed this château himself in the Flemish neo-Renaissance style. Richly decorated by its creator, the château was symbolic of the tastes of the triumphant bourgeoisie of the late 19th century.

In 1933, the château became the private residence of Paul Van Zeeland, Belgian Prime Minister in the inter-war period. The château suffered two fires during the 1980s and was then abandoned for thirty years. Time, thieves and vandals have done the rest.

Its belated classification by the Monument and Sites Directorate did nothing to change the situation. The site was recently purchased by a very wealthy Spaniard of noble descent, Don Luis Fidalgo, with the intention of transforming it into a second home for his family. After extensive renovation work completed in 2014, Château Charle-Albert and its adjacent grounds have regained their former glory.

295. — Boitsfort — Château Charles-Albert.
Photo, La Cartophilie Belge, Bruxelles.

A WALK THROUGH
LE COIN DU BALAI

Boitsfort between Balai and the forest

Rue de la Cigale (between No. 58 and 60 of Rue Middelbourg), Krikelenberg, Rue du Grand Veneur, Drève de Bonne Odeur, Rue Eigenhuis, Place Rik Wouters, Rue de la Sapinière, Rue du Rouge-Gorge, Chaussée de la Hulpe, Rue Middelbourg
Tram No. 94 or bus No. 95, Wiener stop; Bus No. 17, Diabolo stop

Made up of little hilly streets bordering the Sonian Forest, the Coin du Balai is difficult to get to. It owes its name, 'Broom Corner', to a legend that tells of how Charles V thanked a local peasant for his hospitality by granting him the exclusive and transmittable privilege to make brooms. Miraculously, this neighbourhood has preserved its village atmosphere thanks to its day labourers and workers' homes, most of which date from the early 20th century. The ambiance here is decisively positive and convivial, or to sum it all up in one word – boitsfortian.

Many of the façades are decorated with charming details that illustrate the love the residents have for their neighbourhood. Here is an original, circular itinerary that will let you fully appreciate its charms. Between No. 58 and 60 rue Middelbourg, take the stairs of rue de la Cigale. You'll end up at Krikelenberg; turn right. On your right, below a château, a paved street leads up the hill. This street, which begins as rue du Grand Veneur before becoming drève de Bonne Odeur, once linked Boitsfort and Hoeilart via the forest. At No. 2, a small farm painted pink that dates from the 18th century still has its wooden lintels. Note the old water pump in the courtyard.

Follow drève de Bonne Odeur into the forest after passing by an old forest keeper's house at the corner of rue du Buis. Take the first path on the right, which continues along the cemetery below, and then take rue Eigenhuis, which is named after the company that built the little houses that line the street. The street climbs sharply to place Rik Wouters, formerly called place de la Citadelle, which is the highest point in the neighbourhood. Fauvist painter Rik Wouters set up his studio here at No. 7 in 1913. Continue on rue de la Sapinière and turn right on rue du Rouge-Gorge. To the right, take chaussée de la Hulpe, the backbone of the neighbourhood. At No. 200, the Théâtre du Méridien has a hillside garden that serves as a stage for exhibitions and plays in the summer. At No. 124–128 rue Middelbourg, the 'casbah' is a strange, eclectic style building (1911–1923) built from architectural elements recuperated after the 1910 World's Fair. At No. 70, take a look through the gate of the chaotic Château of Jolymont, whose origins date back to the 16th century.

DOMAINE DES SILEX ⑦

A huge open-air aviary

Chemin des Silex (at the signs indicating the estate)
02 672 88 03 – cowb.be – info@cowbe.be
Saturday 9am–6pm, and the first Sunday of the month 9am–12pm
Free guided tour on the first Sunday of the month at 9.30am (booking not required)
Tour begins at the corner of the chemin des Silex and avenue de la Foresterie
Tram No. 94 or bus No. 95, Wiener stop; Bus No. 17, Étangs de Boitsfort stop

Few know of the Domaine des Silex, a surprising site caught between two of Brussels' largest natural areas: the Sonian Forest and Tournay-Solvay Park. This small 4 hectare estate was bought by Leopold II himself in 1901, in an attempt to protect the beauty and tranquility of the Vuylsbeek valley, which was threatened by the urbanization of Boitsfort. Now a property of the Royal Trust, the estate has been run by the Commission Ornithologique de Watermael-Boitsfort (COWB, Watermael-Boitsfort Ornithological Commission) and the Brussels Environment Organization since 1999. They have worked to restore and strengthen the site's biodiversity, which explains why they are hesitant about opening the site to visitors more often.

The estate is organized around a large rectangular and artificial pond that was once devoted to fishing. An alley of ancient thujas leads to the pond. Old chestnut trees and a few conifers that may have been planted during the time of Leopold lightly contrast with the indigenous vegetation that has recently been reintroduced (reedy marsh, orchard, saplings, etc.) and that is given special treatment (mowing and trimming techniques are adapted to each plant, the riverbanks are laid out in such a way as to protect the plants, etc.). The result is a unique natural environment that is rare in Brussels, where reed warblers, common and green sandpipers, and a few bat species have taken up residence again. But that's not all: 153 species of bird inhabit this site, transforming the pond into an open-air aviary. If chirping isn't your cup of tea, you have two options: take a bird tour led by a specialist on the first Sunday of every month, or spend some time relaxing beneath one of the orchard's apple trees.

HEAD OFFICE OF CIMENTERIES ET BRIQUETERIES RÉUNIES (CBR)

A reminiscence of James Bond, the Space Race, and Marilyn's lips

Chaussée de la Hulpe 185
Tram No. 94, Coccinelles stop

© Jean-Jacques Evrard

Built in 1967, this building combines everything Sixties with elements reminiscent of James Bond, the Space Race, and Marilyn's lips. But there's also a little something extra that defies categorization, a feeling of strangeness and haunting beauty. In bright white, the ghost-like shape bursts out. This building, the main headquarters of CBR (a cement and brick company), had to glorify the technical and expressive potential of concrete. The architect, Constantin Brodzki, thus started with a prefabricated, moulded motif that he repeated over and over again on the façades of the two connected structures. If you are rather discreet about it, you can try to get a look at the lobby during office hours.

The entrance, whose location is not indicated in any shape or form, blends perfectly into the façade. Inside, the proportions are surprising – large beneath low ceilings – as is the contrast of the materials used: washed concrete, wooden frames accentuating the 'portholes', and a parquet floor made from standing timber. Note the entrance to the basement, which is nothing but a barely noticeable hole encircled by a narrow steel railing. Contemporary artwork also decorates the space.

NEARBY
Head office of the Glaverbel Company ⑨

Chaussée de la Hulpe 166
Tram No. 94, Coccinelles stop

In the 1960s, Glaverbel was one of the first large companies to leave the city centre for the suburbs of Brussels. This decision would leave its mark and lead to a sharp rise in the development of tertiary architecture along chaussée de la Hulpe and boulevard du Souverain. The building, which soon became a landmark, was the work of a team of architects consisting of Renaat Braem, André Jacqmain, Victor Mulpas and Pierre Guillisen. In an exceedingly stunning manner, the façades blend the roughest of materials, badly quarried blue stone, with glass.

This union of opposites is celebrated in the very form of the building: a large ring. In correlation with the nearby forest, the surrounding nature is glorified both outside the building, by the reflective façades, and inside, by the actual park found at the centre of the structure. During office hours, you can enter on the ground floor and take a walk around this large, enclosed garden that redefines the common relationship between the interior and the exterior.

FORMER BOITSFORT RACECOURSE

A nine-hole golf course in the middle of the city

Chaussée de la Hulpe 53A
Tram No. 94, Hippodrome de Boitsfort stop

© Jean-Jacques Evrard